TURNING POINT
REACHING IN ME... TO FIND ME...

© 2010 Godzchild, Inc.

Published by Godzchild Publications
a division of Godzchild, Inc.
22 Halleck St., Newark, NJ 07104
www.godzchildproductions.net

Printed in the United States of America 2010— First Edition
Book Cover designed by Stephen Reid of Chosen Grfx

All rights reserved. No part of this publication may be reproduced, stored in a retrieval system, or transmitted in any form or by any means – for example, electronic, photocopy, recording – without the prior permission of the publisher. The only exception is brief quotations in printed reviews.

> Library of Congress Cataloging-in-Publications Data
> Turning Point: Reaching In Me To Find Me/Kevin Willians.
> Includes bibliographical references and scriptural references.
> ISBN 978-0-9840955-2-0   (pbk.)
> 1. Williams, Kevin. 2. Empowerment. 3. Christianity.

2010927059

Unless otherwise indicated, Scripture quotations are from the King James Version of the Bible

TABLE OF CONTENTS

TURNING POINT
Reaching In Me... To Find Me...

DECISIONS
Chapter 1: *This is Where I Pivot*..3
Chapter 2: *Tomorrow's Success Depends on Today's Decision*..........9
Chapter 3: *Why is the Question; Why Not is the Answer*................13
Chapter 4: *Plan to Succeed*..17
Chapter 5: *Stick to the Source*..21
Chapter 6: *Deliver Yourself from You!*...25
Chapter 7: *Bring Your Valley with You!*.......................................29

PERCEPTIONS
Chapter 8: *Perception Makes all the Difference*............................35
Chapter 9: *Know Who You Are!*..39
Chapter 10: *Do You Have Enough Information?*..........................43
Chapter 11: *Don't Run for the New; Just Dig Deeper*....................47
Chapter 12: *Embrace Your Doubt*...51
Chapter 13: *The Blind Side of Perception*....................................55
Chapter 14: *Believe Beyond Your Ability*.....................................59

CHALLENGES
Chapter 15: *Accept Every Challenge*..65
Chapter 16: *Anything Not Challenged Will Remain Permanent*......69
Chapter 17: *Raise Your Standard*..73
Chapter 18: *Reaching Unity*...77
Chapter 19: *The Problem with Procrastination*............................81
Chapter 20: *The Real GIANT is Your Vision*.................................85
Chapter 21: *Challenged to Be Content*..89

Reinvent Yourself
Chapter 22: *Reinventing You*..*95*
Chapter 23: *Study Your Audience!*...*99*
Chapter 24: *Fear Ain't Always a Bad Thing*.......................................*103*
Chapter 25: *Find Your "Good Place"*..*107*
Chapter 26: *Who are Your Influences?*...*111*
Chapter 27: *Never Let Anyone Gamble With Your Future*...............*115*
Chapter 28: *Nothing is Ever Simple*..*119*

Now What?
Chapter 29: *Be True to Your Commitment*..*125*
Chapter 30: *Be Self-Motivated*...*129*
Chapter 31: *Be a Progressive Visionary*..*133*
Chapter 32: *Be Balanced*..*137*
Chapter 33: *Be Disciplined*..*141*
Chapter 34: *Be Healthy and Rest!*...*145*
Chapter 35: *Be a Dreamer*..*149*

~To my father, the late Bishop Frank Williams; my mother, Mother Florence Williams; my brother, Michael Williams; and to two of the greatest churches on this side of heaven--Monument of Praise Ministries and New Jerusalem Cathedral.

Decisions

Chapter One

This is Where I Pivot

"You don't have to see the whole staircase; just take the first step."
-*Dr. Martin Luther King Jr.*

You have opened this book because you want to make a change. You've been yearning for something different, fresh and new. This first section will help you to make conscious and godly decisions that will not only affect and benefit your life, but will also affect and benefit the lives of those around you.

Now, whenever you hear the name Christopher Reeve, what images come to mind? Well, chances are, if I asked you this question before 1994, I am sure you would say *Superman*. *Superman*—we all know who he is. He is the one and only indisputable superhero with super strength and super powers. He has the power to fly and the power to switch roles in the blink of an eye. Reeve's portrayal of *Superman* was an inspiration to anyone who ever had a dream to become bigger than their traditional 9-5 job.

And then Christopher Reeve experienced "the turn." He had a face-to-face confrontation with catastrophe. It was a devastating and tragic turn that happened in 1994, after a horseback riding accident left Christopher "Superman" Reeve paralyzed for life, from the neck down. His dreams quickly vanished. His life suddenly shifted. The bottom fell out from beneath him and he was left with a decision to make.

Do I live or do I die?
Do I keep fighting or do I allow this accident to alter my future forever?

Turning Point

I'm sure, like many of us, Reeve wanted to give up. I'm certain He wanted to let go. Reports indicate that he spoke to his doctors and asked them to remove him from life support so that he could end his depression and die a painful and unbearable death. But his wife overruled his decision and asked the doctors to grant Reeve two more years to live.

Reeve didn't know it at the time, but those two years of extended life literally changed his purpose and passion forever.

I begin with this story because I believe that eventually, every human being will get to a point in their journey where they realize, "It's time for me to make a change. It's time for my company to take a risk. It's time for my family to take a leap of faith." That time has come for you. The time is now. You've got to decide and you've got to turn. I recommend you do it now before you end up regretting this chapter in your life.

> *Good information can save you from years and years of student loan debt and unnecessary coursework.*

Like Reeve, some of us are forced to decide after a death occurs in the family or after we lose our jobs, while others are prone to just move out on faith because we have a high level of instinct and discernment. Whatever the reason you've chosen to make the turn—whether it is a financial turn, a relational turn, or a spiritual turn—you must first be willing to store up as much good information as you can get your hands on, so that your decision isn't emotional and temporary. Good information is better than good credit. Good information can save you from years and years of student loan debt and unnecessary coursework. Good information comes in all shapes and sizes. A businessman or a businesswoman without good information and a solid plan will soon find themselves drowning in debt due to poor financial management. An anxious parent who does not think about the pros and cons of having children could end up losing their child to the system, all because they did not receive good information, or put themselves in a place to learn the necessary steps toward success.

So where do we begin? How do we begin? We begin with decisions. And not just decisions, but we must step toward *good* decision-making skills. The first step toward a good decision is the ability to declare to yourself: I will not allow anything or anyone in my life to keep me bound any longer; not even me. And then you've got to choose to keep living even in the face of death; in the face of defeat; in the face of failure. Make a declaration to yourself that, "I will not be in this same situation next year, next month, or next week." I can't. I won't. I will not. And after you've made this declaration, keep your promise.

> *You probably know what it feels like to live, but you also know that you're not living like God said you should live.*

The second step you must take will require you to cross over the bridge between doing the norm and living your dream. All of us who are serious about making the turn will cross this bridge of difficult decisions because this particular road will take us from average life to abundant life. It will take us from ordinary life to an extraordinary standard of living. You probably know what it feels like to live, but you also know that you're not living like God said you should live. You know what it's like to pass through life or allow life to pass you by, but the truth of the matter is, you're not living like your Spirit is telling you that you should live. Sure, you have done pretty well. You have had some accomplishments happen in life. But deep within your spirit, you know and I know that there is more water to draw from your well of life. Why? Because you are a dreamer. You are a visionary. You are more than a conqueror. And you have a desire to do more than what other people can perceive you capable of doing.

So...here we are. You're at the place where you have realized: "this is where I pivot." This is where I change directions. This is where I move out and do something different. But

Turning Point

changing directions is only half of the decision process. Whenever you pivot, you actually allow an imbalance to take place in your life. You literally allow a bit of chaos and discomfort. You welcome trials and you welcome tribulation into your life, because any time a real turn takes place, it is ultimately the imbalance that will bring about a better balance in the end.

Let me say it like this: If you know anything about dance, you know that a solid pivot happens whenever your left foot turns in the opposite direction of your right foot. Your two feet meet for a short period of time, but their first meeting is awkward. It feels a bit unstable. You feel as if your equilibrium is off. But then, all of a sudden, you realize: "I'm not going in the same direction anymore. I'm not thinking about the same things anymore. I'm not making the same decisions anymore." Why? Because you have decided to pivot. You have pivoted past your fears. You have pivoted beyond the pressure of family, friends, or familiar territory. And pivoting is the true evidence that you have *decided* to make the turn. You have pivoted, and therefore, you have made a good decision because when you look up, you realize that you're still standing on your two feet even though you are heading in a different direction.

This is good news, and this is a great start. But, the only way to arrive to this point of departure, you must learn to become comfortable with uneasiness. Uneasiness is not a sign of instability. It is a sign of faith. It is not a sign of weakness. It is actually a sign of strength in God's everlasting power and not your finite plans.

I realize this may not make much sense to you now, but true balance comes in instability. Strength comes in weakness. Healing comes out of sickness. Prosperity comes out of poverty. So, riding the horse will not help you to make the turn; it's actually the moment you fall off that causes the wheel of decision-making to begin turning.

Balance comes in instability. Decisions come with good information. As you begin to turn, learn to be comfortable with feeling uneasy. If you think about it, your right and left foot are never really straight even when you're walking around from day to day. The truth is, they are imbalanced to bring you balance. As well, your small toe is not so much designed to help you look pretty or to have nice toenail polish. It's actually designed to balance the rest of you.

Christopher Reeve learned to see his "imbalance" as an inspiration for all of those who are suffering just like him. Before he passed away, he published a best-selling book called *Nothing is Impossible*; and whether he knew it or not, he was quoting Scripture. Luke 1:37 states, "For with God, nothing shall be impossible." No doubt, nothing is impossible for you! Just believe that God is lord over your decisions, and be bold enough to bounce back from whatever tragic accident you may have encountered.

> *This is where you pivot. This is where you shift. No turning back now.*

CHAPTER TWO

Tomorrow's Success Depends on Today's Decision

"In a moment of decision, the best thing you can do is the right thing to do. The worst thing you can do is nothing."
-*Theodore Roosevelt*

Tomorrow's success depends on today's decision. That's a little slogan I often say to the members of my church. I even find myself repeating these words to myself because if I don't keep them in my mind, I will sink my ship of success by sailing on the fantasy of a lie. What I mean is this: most times, we think success is going to come out of the sky and drop on our front door. We think that after we shout and dance in church or after we attend a conference with the greatest motivational speakers, that blank checks will be shipped to our house overnight. We fall in love with a lie. And because we fall in love with a lie, we end up married to an idea of success that isn't real. It's a fantasy. It is fiction. And more people will buy into fiction before they accept the facts. If you don't believe it, take a walk over to the nearest bookstore around. Fiction is one of the most popular genres of literary documentation because millions of people love to make up stories about themselves. Or they love to read made-up stories about someone else. So they will put a down payment on good luck or depend on a hot lottery ticket to pay off old debts, when the truth of the matter is, 98% percent of success stories don't happen in a day. They happen with a decision. They happen with a deliberate choice to make the turn.

If you are serious about succeeding, then there are two essential ingredients to every successful recipe. First, you must decide and act at the same time. Why? Because deciding and

Turning Point

acting are one phase, not two. You can't make a decision without acting toward it. And you can't act toward anything without the determination it takes to shift from neutral to drive. You know this already, but most of us don't stop to really think about it. No car is in motion until the driver inserts the key into the ignition, cranks up the vehicle, and maneuvers the gears from park to drive. And interestingly enough, especially with an automatic transmission, you've got to go down a series of shifts before you get to drive. You start at the parked position—everyone starts at a parked position—but after you move from park, you have a few options available to you. You can opt to shift down one level to reverse—which is what many of us do every time we say, "I'm not good enough for this or that." Or you have the option of hanging out in neutral. But just remember, if you are in neutral, the only thing your car is good for is a push. It has no stamina or independence of its own. Someone will always have to stand behind you or signal in front of you every step of the way just to make sure that you get to your destination.

> *Anyone who finds themselves deciding on something without acting on it, is just thinking. They aren't moving.*

Aren't you tired of being pushed around? Aren't you done with the neutral norms? Don't you realize that your vehicle's worth is far more valuable to God than a provisional push around the park? If you really saw yourself greater than neutral, you would push past the easy options and get to the drive shift today—right now!

You must act. You must decide. Anyone who finds themselves deciding on something without acting on it, is just thinking. They aren't moving. They're just thinking. And if you're just thinking, you're not progressing. You're not doing anything different than what you did before. There is no destination point in view, no course of action to explore; nothing. You're just brainstorming ideas. Your paper hasn't been submitted to the teacher. Your supervisor hasn't even accepted your proposal. At this point, you're doing initial research on the internet trying to find the best topic to write about.

Real decisions happen because you've accompanied your thoughts with visible actions. Another example is that of swinging a bat. You can't swing a bat and hit the ball without following through. The follow-through is what gets you to first base; not putting on the uniform or whispering a cute prayer before going out on the field. The follow-through is what gives validity to your choice to swing in the first place, not your lofty young-minded dreams of one day becoming a baseball player. You've got to follow through.

The second crucial ingredient involves valuing your time. If you are going to turn toward success, you must realize how important time is. You can pretend you're an immortal being if you want, but time is of the essence. Time is everything. In just ten more years, you may be eligible for retirement. Why sit there another day working a shift that you should be in charge of yourself? Why quit school just for the temporary pleasure of not having to study or write, when your education could open the door to the greatest opportunities you could ever imagine? You can't continue to waste time like this. Sitting on the internet, reading the latest gossip magazines, watching T.V for hours on end—if you want to be successful, you've got to put a limit on your idle time. Put a lid on your laziness and stop using a new episode or a newsflash as your excuse to stay mediocre. Successful people who are serious about changing their present status (economically, socially, or spiritually) are conscientious of the time they invest in any given project, plan, or idea. Can you say the same about yourself?

This was the secret behind Abraham's successful voyage to prosperity. He continued to increase in prosperity not because he

> *If you are going to turn toward success, you must realize how important time is.*

was the smartest man around or because his idea was the best in town; but he was able to move quickly and he was able to make decisions. In Genesis 12:1, Abraham *decides* to obey. He *decides* to relocate. He shows God (at seventy-five years of age) that he means business by leaving familiar territory and risking it all for the sake of God's blessing. He doesn't have a blueprint in front of him but he has a plan inside of Him. His mission statement is: obedience at all costs, no matter how uncomfortable. That is his plan and he sticks to it; even after God asks him to sacrifice Isaac in Genesis 22, he sticks to the plan. He maintains motion. He receives instructions from God, and with urgency and determination, he sets out to do what he is asked to do. Of course we know that God is testing Abraham to see his level of faithfulness, but the point I want to make is that Abraham takes decision-making seriously. He also values his time and God's time. He doesn't tarry for months like most of us do, thinking about the best way to tell Sarah. He doesn't run around town asking a million people for the best company name that he should go with. No! He just builds his decisions off of a strong foundation of faith. He shifts his automatic from park to drive. He models the attitude we need to exude as we move today toward whatever dreams we want to obtain tomorrow.

> *Why are you still in neutral?*
> *Tomorrow's success depends on today's decision.*

CHAPTER THREE

Why is the Question; Why not is the Answer

"There are no foolish questions and no man becomes a fool until he has stopped asking questions."
-Charles Proteus Steinmetz

When I was in college, I had a big issue with one of my professors. I was angry with him after he gave us a final exam with just three questions on it. First of all, three questions meant I had a lot of work to do. I had to give thorough answers for each question and I had to incorporate any and all creative ideas that I could conjure into this examination. If I did not do so, I would not pass the exam. Well, everyone who took the test stayed for about two hours working long and hard to answer the questions posed to us.

Everyone except one student.

After about twenty minutes, a guy in the front of class stood up, turned in his paper, and walked out of the room. I assumed he didn't study. "No sense in pretending you know something when you don't know it," I thought to myself as I nodded my head. If I were him, I would've left, too. But I wasn't him. I was an A student. I wasn't a quitter. So I stayed for about an hour longer, and after I turned in my test, I thought for sure that my hand would need corrective surgery. It nearly fell off after writing so much information down on paper! I was tired. I was weak. I was worn. But I was glad to be done, and I had answered as efficiently as possible. I was ready to get my A.

That didn't happen. When I received my grade, it ended up being lower than the student who walked out in twenty minutes! He got an A. I got a B. *I was hot. I was steaming. I was overheating.*

Turning Point

I had given a complete essay answer, but the student who received an A, responded to one of the questions in two simple words: "Why not?" That was his answer: Why not?

Can you believe it? "Why not" was the answer he gave and the teacher graded him higher than me!

When I went over to inquire about this, my teacher turned to me and said, "Williams, sometimes you've got to learn that there is no reason for you to stay where you are. Your "why not" may be the best answer you can give."

I'll never forget this lesson and I hope you won't either. You need to know that WHY is the question, but WHY NOT is the answer. You may be wasting precious time trying to put together the best plan or you may be spending days and days trying to write the best essay, but the truth is, you might produce an A paper with your "Why not" instead of your long dissertation that no one will never read. Your WHY NOT has the ability to change everything. Your WHY NOT will give you the motivation you need to move out of neutral. Your WHY NOT can give you a mission statement for your next turn in life. Why not see success before you turn forty? Why not go back to school? Why NOT become an entrepreneur? Why NOT try again? WHY is the question...Why not is the answer!

> *Your WHY NOT has the ability to change everything.*

Now let me insert a quick disclaimer: I do not condone writing two word answers on tests. I am NOT advising you to choose an easier route and avoid the discipline of study and preparation. What I am saying is, your answer *might* be found in the questions you ask. In Numbers 13. Joshua and Caleb were bold enough to ask the right questions. Caleb determined, "Let us go up at once and take possession, for we are well able to overcome it." But the men who went up with him replied, "We are not able to go up against the people, for they are stronger than we." Ten spies responded in fear. Joshua and Caleb moved by faith. In the end, Joshua and Caleb were able to enter into the land flowing with milk and honey...all because they responded, "WHY NOT?"

Doubt will try to bind you, and insecurity will try to imprison you, but you have the power to succeed. The Promised Land has your name on it. Milk and honey are waiting for you to move toward Canaan. The vision can only be carried out by you. I know people are around you who think you can never be great. There maybe "classmates" around who think you will never earn an A, but learn to ignore the doubters, pray for the haters, and make the turn.

The ten other spies saw the strength of their opposition externally. They only focused on the physical differences between them and the people blocking them. Joshua and Caleb saw the strength of their God. They learned to focus on what they could not see, and place more interest in what God was able to do beyond their ability to do it themselves. You need to do the same. Learn to focus on what you see in your mind and not what your mind tells you to see. Set your affection on things above and not on things of this world. Why? Because when what is in my head is bigger than what I see opposing me, I can make better decisions. I can run toward what God is leading me to possess, instead of delaying what God has stored up for me.

> *Learn to focus on what you see in your mind, and not what your mind tells you to see.*

You have nothing holding you back from this turn. WHY NOT make it now? WHY NOT move forward with the plan? WHY NOT walk out of the classroom with your head up and your chest out? There is no reason for you to stay where you are. There is too much at stake for you to sit still and sit back on this one. It's time to bring that vision into fruition. Make the turn. Make the change. Make a move.

The Promised Land has already been promised. Now, it's time for you to possess it.

Chapter Four

Plan to Succeed

"You can always amend a big plan, but you can never expand a little one. I don't believe in little plans. I believe in plans big enough to meet a situation which we can't possibly foresee now."
-*Harry S. Truman*

If you love ice cream, then I'm sure you'll love this. It was Ben Cohen and Jerry Greenfield, the now-legendary duo, who decided to open a business years ago after taking a correspondence course on the art of ice cream making. I'm sure people around them thought, "You two are fools for deciding to study ice cream making. No one strikes it rich from ice cream." But despite the odds, they pressed on, received good information, and soon discovered an open door of opportunity for them.

A small college town in Burlington, Vermont did not have an ice cream shop. There was a little gas station on the corner that could easily become the headquarters for their invention. So they put their minds together, put their money together, and with $8,000 in savings and a $4,000 loan, Ben and Jerry leased an old gas station in Burlington, purchased the necessary equipment, and began coming up with ideas for "unique" flavors.

Twenty years later, the company is bringing in over $237 million in annual revenue.

If you want to make the turn, then you must plan to succeed. You must focus on what you believe God is leading you to do, and move past the naysayers and complainers. In addition, the challenge you will face as you make right decisions is two-fold. On the one hand, you must make up in your mind that you are not just going to maintain success, but you are going to be better because of your success. This small principle is important because you are not just making the change because you have nothing else better to do. Rather, you are deciding to change your entire outlook and presentation by making this change. You are going to aim high and dream big, or you might as well not aim at all.

Regardless of what you are aiming for—if you want a successful marriage, a prosperous business, a booming career; if you want to graduate with honors or maybe God has given you an invention of some sort—whatever it is, you must not allow yourself to venture out onto the hills of success without a plan. It is the plan that ensures that your vision will last. It is your plan that will drive your passion. Without a vision, the people perish. Without a plan, the dream will die.

> *Regardless of what you are aiming for...you must not allow yourself to venture out onto the hills of success without a plan.*

The Bible reveals to us various episodes in which someone had a plan, executed that plan, and gained success as a result of it. Nehemiah 1:1 reveals that in the month of Chisleu, or in the month of December, God was setting up Nehemiah for the best opportunity of his life. Nehemiah had been serving as a cupbearer for the king (Nehemiah 1:1), and during his time there, he was able to learn about the burden of the men of Judah. Nehemiah 1:3 tells us that "the remnant...are in great affliction and reproach: the wall of Jerusalem also is broken down, and the gates are burned with fire." In that very instant, God had put Nehemiah in a position that he didn't realize he would be in. Like many of us, Nehemiah knew that God had something great for him, even though he did not know how God was going to do it. Instead of moving too quickly, Nehemiah prayed on behalf of the people and waited until God revealed the right time for him to speak to the king. If you continue reading the book of Nehemiah, you'll discover that Chapter 2 opens with these words, "It came to pass in the month of Nissan." Nissan is the month of April. Chisleu was the month of December. This means that Nehemiah waited for four months before he said a word to the king. God gave him a plan in the month of Chisleu, but the plan wasn't executed until the month of Nissan.

What does this teach us about decision-making? It teaches us a few things. First, when God gives you a vision, do not think that you can go out the next day and do it. You need time to plan it. You need time to mature it. Why? Because the plan that God gives can either become your lifesaver or your destruction. When you wait on a plan, you give yourself time to grow up even as your plan, vision, or dream grows up.

You cannot base good decisions on your level of excitement. Motivation is great, but you've got to have a plan. In addition, the bigger the plan, the more research you'll have to do. The bigger the vision is, the more you'll have to plan for it. As you study this plan, also remember that you will have to study the people, the periphery and anything else attached to the plan. Ben and Jerry had to assess the land, remove any pollutants that reminded buyers of the gas station that once existed there, and they had to save up for their investment. The same is true for us. We have to be spiritually in tune enough to see the opportunities that God is opening up so that we can embrace them and go after them with vitality, with zeal, and with vigor. If we are not prepared for success in our spirit, then we will never be prepared for success in our flesh.

> *If we are not prepared for success in our spirit, then we will never be prepared for success in our flesh.*

Nehemiah and Ben & Jerry had one thing in common: they had a plan. These guys did not just rely on a wing and a prayer. They saved up a few thousand dollars and they did enough homework to predict their success before it even manifested. Nehemiah did the same. He knew that God was setting him up to restore Judah and build the wall, but God granted him favor with the king (as a cupbearer) that eventually opened the door to one of the greatest stories of restoration ever told in Scripture.

What I'm trying to say is simple: get yourself a plan. Study your plan. No one ever just happens to fall into success. They plan to succeed.

CHAPTER FIVE

Stick to the Source!
"Don't climb a tree to look for fish."
-*Author Unknown*

President Barack Obama is a trailblazer for many reasons. Not only is he the first African-American President of the United States of America, but Obama changed the course of political campaigning forever. He wasn't afraid to make different decisions. He wasn't afraid to go against the grain. Before his campaign, no one utilized the internet the way he did. No one realized the impact that the World Wide Web had on the political landscape and the American people. So, Obama capitalized on people's untapped ideas. He created an idea that had never before been thought up. He began circulating information about his goals and dreams via internet, and then he figured out an easy way to accept financial donations. It was a genius idea and an effective plan. And today, everyone in politics is asking the question: "What is the source of Obama's success?"

I'll tell you what his source was. Barack Obama was innovative. He was determined. Barack Obama was an amazing decision maker. He made a decision to go against the code, to go against the popular way of doing business-as-usual, and most importantly, he stuck to what was working for him at the time.

The question you must answer now is, "Am I as determined to carry out my dream after I make the right decisions?" Are you determined to stick to the source after you make it big, or will you change up on God after He brings you into prosperity? Every decision-maker needs to remember the importance of staying connected to your source. For Christians, that source is God. For others, your source may be your family. But, whatever the source is, staying connected to it is more important than houses, cars, or any other earthly possession you may one day acquire.

Why do I say this? I say it because your source invigorates you and motivates you to keep working even when you are tired. Your source will encourage you to push past fear and dismiss all worry if ever you find that your ideas haven't harvested good success immediately. The truth of the matter is, God is not going to work with anyone that does not want to work. If God is your source, and God is the reason you are doing what you are doing, then God wants to make sure that anything that he is investing in, is going to produce; anything that He speaks to is going to produce. Therefore, we stay connected to Him because otherwise, we wouldn't be able to produce anything abundant outside of Him.

> *...we stay connected to Him because otherwise, we wouldn't be able to produce anything abundant outside of Him.*

Let me prove it to you in Scripture. In the beginning of time, during the creation narrative, God spoke to everything He made and told it to bring forth more of its kind. In Genesis 1:11, we find these words: "And God said, Let the earth bring forth grass, the herb yielding seed, and the fruit tree yielding fruit after his kind, whose seed is in itself, upon the earth: and it was so." In other words, God told the ground "Bring forth of your kind," and since the source of grass, trees, and herbs was somewhere deep in the seeds of the earth, the earth was able to produce of itself.

Later in Genesis 1:20-21, God said, "Let the waters bring forth abundantly the moving creature that hath life, and fowl that may fly above the earth, in the open firmament of heaven. And God created great whales, and every living creature that moveth, which the waters brought forth abundantly, after their kind, and every winged fowl after his kind: and God saw that it was good." Again we see how God told the ocean to "bring forth of your kind," and immediately, it started to produce of itself. The whales and swimming creatures of the ocean understood who their source was. If a fish disconnected itself from the source of its life, there would be no possibility for life. The same is true for those of us who are seeking success. The Lord speaks to us as people of God and we must produce of ourselves. We must work and be diligent in all that we do. Above that, everything we do must be connected to the source. The operation, the strength, and the success that God is going to give you, must be connected to the source. If it is not connected to its source, it will die.

God made us in his image and his likeness (Genesis 1:27). Therefore, our source is not the ground or the water; our source is Him. Our source is the one who created the ground and the ocean over which we have been called to rule. And because our source is Him, we cannot look for success outside of Him. We cannot search for prosperity outside of the God who called us to prosper. Anytime we try to look for success outside of God, we end up digressing. We end up deviating from the plan of God for our lives and we end up unsuccessful. If you don't believe me, ask a few of the wealthy people out there who are wealthy, but empty. They are rich and famous but they feel all alone. And the reason they are empty and lonely is because they thought that an amount of money would give them success, or a career, or a family name, and still they find themselves empty. Read the newspaper. Every year, we have multi-millionaires who have everything to live for, and yet they commit suicide all because they went after something or someone, thinking that he or she would make them happy, and realized later that the money, the man or the woman was not their source. It did not fulfill them. So now, these wealthy people have us ordinary people envying their materials, but in the meantime, the wealthy folk are actually envying our happiness.

> *Anytime we try to look for success outside of God, we end up digressing… and… unsuccessful.*

——— *Stick to the Source!* ———

God is the source of your success campaign. Stay connected to the source. Don't be tricked into falling for the "bling" of success, or the kind of success that deviates you from the plan of God. If you stay connected, you will produce abundantly every time.

Decide to stay connected.

CHAPTER SIX

Deliver Yourself from YOU!

"If you don't like something, change it. If you can't change it, change your attitude."
-Maya Angelou

Mike Tyson was the first ever heavyweight champion to hold the WBA, WBC and IBF titles simultaneously. "Iron Mike" was and is considered to be amongst the greatest heavyweight boxers of all time. During his boxing career, Tyson received over 30 million dollars for several of his fights and accumulated a total of $300 million during his career.

Today, Tyson is broke, busted, and disgusted. In 2003, Tyson filed for bankruptcy and in May 2010, while on the talk show *The View*, Tyson revealed that he is now forced to live paycheck to paycheck. He went on to say: "I'm totally destitute and broke. I have an awesome life, I have an awesome wife who cares about me. Yet, I'm totally broke."

Most of us who have never had $300 million might ask ourselves: "How did Tyson allow this to happen to himself? What went wrong?" And if you're anything like me, you're wondering: "What did you waste all of that money buying?" But, if you know anything about Tyson's personal life—the abusive relationships, the rape conviction and the prison sentence, you'll quickly figure out a very sad truth. The truth is this: one second, you can find yourself on top of the world, and the very next second, you can be checking into a homeless shelter. One second you may find yourself in the best relationship you could've ever imagined, and the very next moment, you are living life as a single parent.

I don't believe Mr. Tyson was a bad guy. I think he is human just like we are all human. The difference, however,

Turning Point

between Tyson's yesterday and our tomorrow depends on our deliverance. I'm not just talking about being delivered from certain habits or cravings. I'm talking about being delivered from yourself. If you are going to make the turn, you've got to decide to deliver yourself from You! If you don't, you may end up like some of the greatest failures of history.

I know you plan to become a manager over a chain of restaurants, or the lead pitcher of a professional baseball team, but before you lead anyone else into deliverance, deliver yourself. Before you can help anyone else get out of debt, get out of debt yourself. Deliver yourself from YOU or the you that you never killed will destroy the YOU that has yet to be discovered. No decision is more important than the decision to examine yourself and change everything about you that is corrupt and cancerous. Before you can be a one-man army, you must be a one man deliverer; and the first person you've got to deliver is YOU. Assess yourself and figure out the potential roadblocks in your life that have come to destroy your future. What is it that the enemy is using as a weapon to assassinate your faith in whatever God said? Is it doubt? Is it fear? If it is, then deliver yourself from doubting yourself. Move away from people who are always making you rethink your first step.

> *Deliver yourself from YOU or the you that you never killed will destroy the YOU that has yet to be discovered.*

What else could you be fearful of? Are you afraid that your mistakes have disqualified you from success? Do you think that God has punished you indefinitely from obtaining the prize simply because you mismanaged a previous season? If you are under this perception, you are sadly mistaken. No mistake you have made up until this point is so big that it will destroy your future. No wrong turn will ever be able to ruin your entire road trip. Just make a U-Turn. Turn around. Only today's delay can destroy tomorrow's destiny. Only if you yield to the power of that mistake, instead of overthrowing it, will you see failure. Your mistake must meet your anointing. Your struggle must meet your Savior.

That's what Jacob's wrestling battle was all about: deliverance from himself (Genesis 32:22-32). He was so caught up in the deceiver that he used to be, that he didn't realize that God's presence had come to help him make the most important turn of his life. The angel wrestled with Jacob so that Jacob could finally deliver himself from a life full of deceit, trickery, and denial. Jacob endured a moment that we all have to deal with: a season of stripping. We must be stripped of the façade that we present to others. We must be stripped of what we used to define ourselves as. We must be stripped of what we used to think was right or wrong; stripped of the justifications; stripped of the excuses we used to make. If we are going to be delivered from ourselves, we've got to endure the stripping that brings about success. Even allow yourself to be stripped of your self-righteous thinking, or your ability to think that you are always right every time. Strip yourself from the sin that keeps you blind, and begin to hunger after what's right. Matthew 5:6 reminds us: "Blessed are they which do hunger and thirst after righteousness: for they shall be filled." If we do not hunger after what is right, then we will pick up excess weight from all of the wrong things; simply because we are snacking on that which is characteristically wrong. We take a comment too far, or we allow someone to tell us "I love you," when they really don't. And sooner or later, we become like "Iron Mike":—abusing or being abused; wasting money or wasting someone else's; living in a "made-up me" and not telling the truth about me!

Decide to be delivered from you. It was after Jacob dealt with himself that God was able to help Jacob deal with the

> *Strip yourself from the sin that keeps you blind, and begin to hunger after what's right.*

Turning Point

unsettled business in his family. In the same way, as you embark upon making this turn, take your deliverance process one day at a time. Rome wasn't built in a day, and the damage done can't be fixed overnight. Just start with YOU. Deliver YOU. Free YOU; so that one day, others can be free because of YOU.

Chapter Seven

Bring Your Valley with You

"Good decisions come from experience, and experience comes from bad decisions."
-Author Unknown

Many people, I have come to realize, are afraid of success. They are afraid to make decisions because of a few bad ones made before. They are afraid to move forward because of the story their history tells. They are afraid to let go of the fear that keeps them living in a world of regret. They are often so discouraged by the past that they never ever move forward. But when you don't move forward, you allow your past to dictate the future. When you don't move forward, you become bitter and full of regret. When you don't move forward, you give your history control over your destiny.

> *...anyone on a mountain today has had a valley experience at some point...*

Don't let it happen.
Don't let the past play the same old sad song again.

You have no reason to stay where you are. Your life has had its many ups and downs, but the truth of the matter is, anyone on a mountain today has had a "valley experience" at some point in his or her life. Anyone you see successful today has had to count up the cost, pay the interest, wipe off the dust from their knees after falling flat on their face, get up, and try again.

We have all been in a valley of sorts, but here is the good news: a valley is only a mountain turned upside down. A valley is only an indicator of how great you can be if the position of your slope changes by 180 degrees. A mountain is an accomplishment today because of the work you had to put into it yesterday. *After* someone climbs to the top successfully, it's all good. The news reporters are interviewing, the family and friends are calling and congratulating, but that does not mean that the top was easily achievable on the first day of climbing.

A mountain of success does not come as a result of one million good decisions. In fact, you may make three good ones out of ten bad attempts, but do you think you should let your negatives overrule the positives? Certainly not! Every move toward success is a necessary one—even the parts of your story that you don't like; even those areas in your life that you are ashamed of, and the chapters that don't seem to fit in with the rest of the plot. It's all necessary for success. It's all necessary for the turn.

The woman with the issue of blood had a valley full of reasons not to leave her home and try Jesus. She was sick for over twelve years. She had exhausted all of her money. She was ostracized, disconnected, and completely ridiculed for an ailment she did not bring upon herself. Not to mention, she was a woman. Her gender, in and of itself, brought its own chain of valley problems, too.

But, this woman was determined to see success. She was determined to turn. If she was anything like some of us, she would've died in the house. She would've stayed on her knees in prayer, hoping for God to just drop a healing package on her front door, and sign it "from heaven to earth." But no, this unnamed woman realized something that many of us are still struggling to understand—and that is this: a mountainous miracle requires mountainous faith. And mountainous faith will make a mountainous miracle.

In other words, if I don't believe that God can make a miracle out of my valley, then I can't expect anything different from what I see right now. I can't expect for change if I am not willing to do anything about my condition. I can't expect prosperity if I continue to adorn myself with layers of doubt, fear,

Bring Your Valley with You

and blame. I can't expect the new if I continue doing the old! I've got to step out of fear, leave the excuses that disqualify me at my bedside, and press through the crowd so that I can climb my way to the mountain where Jesus is.

This is what *Turning Point* is all about. It is the point that you decide not to let your valley hinder your velocity; this is the turning point. When you stop allowing your lows to dictate your luxury, but you motivate yourself by remembering how God has brought you over in times past. This is the turning point. When you refuse to allow low expectations to control God's high interceptions. Do you see the point? You have a mountainous idea in you and God wants to manifest it out of you. You have greatness ahead of you and your future is waiting on you! So let God do what God wants to do. If you think you have no right to the top because of your bottom, I want you to know that you are the best candidate for success. In reality, your lows are indicators of how high your potential really is. In other words, as low as a person has gone and can go, that is the measuring stick for how high that person has the capacity to go.

> *As low as a person has gone, that it the measuring stick for how high that person has the capacity to go.*

Thus, the big question is: What's stopping you? What's holding you back from making the best decision of your life? If your valley can't stop you, then what else can? If your mountain can't move you, then what else will? Who else can? Who has the power to control your life, but you? When has God ever left you out there to fail and to be humiliated? What is stopping you?

Nothing—that's the answer. Nothing is stopping you. The reason nothing can stop you now is because everything you are concerned about, and everything you've wasted time fearing over about tomorrow, you have already experienced yesterday. Think about it. You already know what hurt feels like; you've already had a taste of failure and betrayal. You've been let down before and

———— Turning Point ————

you've been misunderstood. So, really, there is nothing you can think of that has the ability to hinder you from success...nothing.

> *Decide to move toward success, and bring your valley with you.*

Perceptions

Chapter Eight

Perception Makes all the Difference
"All our knowledge is the offspring of our perceptions."
-Leonardo Da Vinci

Have you ever laughed at someone because they thought they knew you and they were completely wrong? Ever listened to someone retell a story about you and by the middle of it, you realized, "This person has mixed up all the actual details and twisted the truth?" If you have, you're not alone. Everyone has experienced it, and the person who told the story was not lying intentionally. They just perceived something about you and then they based their perception on a wrong interpretation or false information.

> *Do you know who you really are? Are you aware of how you are perceived?*

It happens to me all the time. People who have never met me will read about me or see pictures of me, and they will then try to perceive me based upon the picture they see. And still, they can't get me. Some say I'm stern, some say I'm a no non-sense kind of guy, and some just say I'm straight up mean. But when they can't get enough information about me from my photo, they decide to come to a church service on Sunday to hear me preach. Now, after church is over, my mother has overheard some of these people respond about what they perceive about me. She tells me that they say things after church like, "Oh! Your son is so comical and nice and all of that..." Meanwhile, she is looking at them with that cynical "Don't be fooled" face. Why? Because my mother knows the REAL me. She knows my authentic person. She knows that sometimes I can be a straight up mess to deal with, and she also knows my strengths. So, others get one side of my personality, and perceive or assume everything about me, but my mother is able to discern who I really am.

> Do you know who you *really* are?
> Are you aware of how you are perceived?
> Does your perception of you match the perception others have about you?

The first section helped us realize that our decisions are based on one thing; and that is, the information we receive. Now I want to take the subject of decisions a step further. I want to suggest to you that every judgment we make is not only based on good or bad information, but also on good or bad perception. To perceive something means that you think a certain way about the information you have received. To perceive is to make assumptions about a person predicated on the stories you have heard or read. You're gathering information based on your view, or your viewing something based on what you've gathered. In the Christian world, the word 'perception' is another spiritual word for discernment. If I perceive something, that also means I am discerning it. And many times, the way I think—whether it is good or bad—has a lot to do with how I see the world and how I understand my vision in relationship to the people around me. It's all connected. Some people perceive bad things all the time. We all know a few people who are always having a bad day. Nothing is going wrong in actuality, but everyone is blamed, and they are just annoying people to be around. Their countenance is sad. Their body language is negative. And their tone of voice is sharp and uninviting. So, when you and your friends decide to go out to eat, all of you are sending text messages to each other saying, "don't invite THEM out to eat with us. You know who THEM is." But why is this so? Why do negative people view the world so negatively? Well, in my opinion, the reason most people live like this is because they have perceived everyone to be their enemy.

Perception Makes all the Difference

They understand the world as a horrible place to live and so, their mind is always looking for confirmation of their false interpretation. They are victims of their own depression. Life has done them wrong one or two times before, and now they can't get over it. As a result, their perception has ruined their reception. Their perception has swallowed up their ability to trust again or love again. They can't see or think right because of the trauma of one tearful experience.

This is why it is imperative that we discuss in this section the various aspects of good perception and bad perception. There is no way you can make the turn without a greater understanding of how perception plays into your decisions, your challenges, and everything else connected to your vision.

> *Your perception is driven by the way you think, and the way one thinks becomes the driving force...*

The Bible says, "As a man thinketh, so is he" (Proverbs 23:7). In other words, your perception is driven by the way you think, and the way one thinks becomes the driving force or the modem of one's perception. What do I mean by that? I mean that if you learn how to use perception to your advantage, you will win every time. Just like in a game of monopoly—isn't it funny how the nice person *always* wins the game? Ever wonder why? I surely have. First, I think those wonderful and nice winners, like me, win the game because people perceive that I am always going to be nice all of the time. So, I use my smile as a strategy to distract them from paying attention. Then, I conquer my opponents (who are usually a few members of the church) all because they bought into my game of perception. My objective was never to be nice. The objective was to monopolize. When they play with me, they forget that I'm not playing as their pastor. I'm playing as their competitor and the goal is to win (not to preach a sermon about it). Hey...that's the reason we call it monopoly!

Turning Point

You can win this game, but you've got to think yourself into success. Perceive yourself as the winner you already are. Perception makes all the difference.

Chapter Nine

Know Who You Are!

"We must not allow other people's limited perceptions to define us."
-Virginia Satir

Denzel Washington and Tom Hanks are two of my favorite actors. They are both great in what they do. Denzel typically plays a good guy in his movies. He's suave, he has swagger, and he's the hero on the block that always saves the day. And Tom Hanks' performance in *Forrest Gump* hooked me for life. I mean, "Life is like a box of chocolates; you never know what you're going to get. Stupid is as stupid does." Classic movie. This guy deserved every award imaginable. Every time Washington or Hanks premiered a new film, I was one of the first viewers in line to see it.

Well one day, I decide to see a movie called *Training Day*. I I enter the movie theater with a preconceived idea or a perception of what Denzel is going to do. I expect him to win the heart of every viewer as the protagonist of the film. I expect him to have one of those tearjerker scenes. But as the movie progresses, Denzel isn't doing what I perceived. His role presents him as evil and manipulative. He's dark and conniving; and the worst part is, he's doing an amazing job acting as the bad guy!

So *here I am*...sitting in the movie theater with a problem. I don't want to let go of my perception of Denzel, so I end up making excuses for him: "He's going to be fine. God is going to get him. Denzel is going to get convicted by the end and he'll come around." Two hours later, the credits are rolling and I am stuck. I'm still there waiting for the deleted scenes to reveal my perception. No matter the fact that people are leaving the theater at this point, I'm still watching the screen and thinking "this guy is going to get out of that car alive, ask Jesus to save him, and he's going to become a missionary for Training Day 2."

It doesn't happen.

The same disappointment came upon me after Tom Hanks starred in the first movie following his stellar performance in *Forrest Gump*. I can't even tell you the name of this movie if you asked, because I have since blocked it out of my memory. All I remember is that Tom Hanks is cursing like a sailor in the film. He and his boys are trying to rob a bank and it just didn't match the Forrest Gump image I had glued in my mind! Apparently, the couple in front of me felt the same way because all throughout the movie, I could hear them mumbling complaints. We never expected to see Hanks in this kind of movie. My feelings were hurt, I felt like writing him a letter. I became a bit emotional. And by the time I left the theater, I thought to myself, "I need a pill."

> *How you perceive something or someone will determine your opinion of that thing.*

Let me tell you what my problem was. I had perceived these two amazing actors to *be* the roles that they were portraying; and I forgot who they *were*. I forgot what they did for a living. I assumed that they would only participate in movies that I was comfortable seeing them in, and I was wrong. Denzel and Tom, if you're reading this: please forgive me! Much love to you both and your amazing craft!

The problem was with my perception. I misjudged their artistry based on a preconceived expectation. It wasn't their fault. In reality, Hanks and Washington *are* actors. This is their job. And they were paid between $5 and $20 million to participate in a film they enjoyed because of the picture it painted; not the story I wanted them to tell.

The same principle applies to our lives and to our perception. How you perceive something or someone will determine your opinion of that thing.

Consider John 12:12-19. Jesus went from local to worldwide

in a week. In John 12:19, the Pharisees say among themselves, "Perceive ye how we prevail nothing? Behold, the world is gone after him." In other words, Jesus was being surrounded by a crowd of people who all seemed to celebrate him for the great deliverer that he was. Lazarus was with him, whom Jesus raised from the dead, and the people were fascinated by this miracle. So they followed him, they perceived certain conclusions about him, and by the next week, the same followers with palms in their hands crying out "Hosana," were the very people crying out, "Crucify Him."

> *It is a dangerous thing to place your perception in the hands of your haters.*

This story tells us something important. It is a dangerous thing to place your perception in the hands of your haters. People's perception of you, or what someone thinks about you, should not become the definition of you in your own dictionary. You should know who you are and know what you are called to do regardless of what people call you, expect of you, or ask you to do. If you know who you are, then you won't allow the crowd to mess up your self-perception. You won't allow people to stop you from filming another movie or becoming a great entrepreneur with different visions and passions.

Perception is key. The more you persevere in the kingdom of God, the more you will be perceived, viewed, and judged by quite a few people. Everyone that you help will not be as appreciative of you as they should. Everyone you try to bring into the plan will not help you the way you would help them. Be like Jesus in John 12. In this situation with the crowd, Jesus knows that everyone doesn't perceive him correctly. Some are celebrating him; others are tolerating him. Some are rejecting him, and others are ostracizing him. Still, it does not change him. Jesus wasn't the type to avoid something just because of what people thought about him. Even in John 8:59, Jesus is being threatened by people who are mad, chaotic and crazy. Scripture says, "Then took they

Turning Point

up stones to cast at him: but Jesus hid himself, and went out of the temple, going through the midst of them, and so passed by." Now, they are getting ready to kill him and Jesus does not even fight or run. He just walks away in the midst of their chaos. And, the reason he can walk away from them is because he understood what we do not yet understand. He understood that his destiny and purpose did not end with a mob trying to kill him. Rather, he had to be crucified, he had to lay down his life and no man would be able to take it.

If you are going to do the work of God and if you want to make this next turn, you must know yourself in and out. Know your purpose and know your vision. Don't let your viewers keep you locked into one character. You are so much more than a one hit wonder.

Know Yourself. Celebrate Yourself. If you don't, no one else will.

Chapter Ten

Do You Have Enough Information?

"Information is a source of learning. But unless it is organized, processed, and available to the right people in a format for decision making, it is a burden, not a benefit."
-William Pollard

Picture this. A man is walking toward you with a knife in his hand. He's disguised in apparel that normal people wouldn't wear everyday. You look to your right. You look to your left. You cannot escape. You cannot hide. You become nervous and afraid.

What are you going to do? How will handle this?

> ↢✧↣
> *Knowing the information is vital to every choice you make on this journey toward success.*

Immediately, I bet you would say, "I'm going to defend myself," or, "This is the end for me." But in all honesty, I haven't given you enough information for you to make an informed decision. Without all of the information, your perception and evaluation is off.

What if I told you the man is a surgeon and the knife he is using is not going to kill you, but instead, it is going to heal you? What if I said the man with the knife is the best chef in town, and the knife he plans to use is necessary to cut into the turkey he prepared for Thanksgiving dinner? The uniform is mandatory for work, so of course it is not customary for every-day apparel. Knowing the information is vital to every choice you make on this journey toward success.

In reality, half of us fail not because we lack determination or drive, but simply because we build our grand ideas on the cement of incorrect information. We build our dreams on quicksand. We want to move quickly, but we've got to have all of the information. Information informs perception. No one told us that the relationship we were about to make permanent, carried a lot of unrevealed baggage. No one told us that the property taxes would increase if we bought commercial property in a certain area. No one warned us about the difference between a fixed rate and an adjustable rate before we purchased our home. So now we are head over heels in debt, all because we didn't take the time to ask, "Do I have enough information?"

In 1 Chronicles 13, David moves the Ark of the Covenant, consults the elders, but he never consults God. Scripture says, "David consulted with the captains of thousands and hundreds, and with every leader. And David said to all of the assembly of Israel, if it seems good to you...let us bring the ark of our God back to us" (1 Chronicles 13:1-3 NKJV), but he never gets permission from God. Yes, he goes to all of the elders in the religious community, and leaders who consult leaders is fine; however, when God gives you instructions and you go against the principle, you will always find yourself making the wrong move. David was disobedient, but the people were just as culpable. The instructions were to carry the Ark on their shoulders. The carriers took it upon themselves to create an ox cart on which to move the Ark. This was strictly forbidden. The people tried to carry the Ark with their own invention. They put the ark on the cart, and as they were moving, the Ark of the Covenant shifted. It looked as if it was about to fall to the ground, and one innocent man lost his life because of a two-fold disobedience. Interestingly enough, they had enough respect for the Ark not to allow it to fall, but they did not respect it enough to carry it the way God commanded them to carry it.

The point is this: if you don't deviate from the principles, it won't cost you your life (or someone you love). Asking good questions and getting the right perception about something is the most important thing to do as you make the turn. Before you turn, assess as much as possible. After you turn, learn as much as you can in order to move forward. Don't just consult the top advisors or the senior officials. Ask God and get it confirmed within your spirit (based on the principles of the Word of God or your foundational beliefs, i.e. bylaws of the corporation, mission statement of your company, etc.). Ask God to show you the important steps to make before you end up running away from the doctor who was brought into your life to heal you.

> *True success happens when you believe that God has given you the information necessary to carry out the vision.*

David isn't the only figure in the Bible who ended up making this mistake. Sarah laughed when God sent messengers to inform her that she and Abraham would have a child in their old age. She had a level of disbelief that could have caused her to miss out on her promise. And even after God read her thoughts, Sarah tried to help God out by having Hagar, her mistress, have a baby by Abraham, her husband. She had all of the information but she didn't trust it; because information without full understanding, leads to bad judgment. She is no different than some person who reads two chapters in a book and assumes they have figured out the plot and conclusion. Just like Sarah, we are excellent starters, but few of us are finishers. All of the resources were within her, but she didn't see her barrenness as a blessing. To her, it was a barrier

Trust what God imparts. See the blessing in the barrenness. True success happens when you believe that God has given you the information and the understanding necessary to carry out the vision. Do you believe God? Do you believe in yourself? Have you received proper instructions from heaven? If so, then move out of the muck and mire of misinformation and begin to build on a sure foundation. Build your success not on the sticks and stones of speculation and guesswork, but build your success on solid ground. Get all of the details. Making an informed decision.

―――― **Turning Point** ――――

Follow your dreams and listen to God, because everything that you dream up does not necessarily mean it has been God-given. You know when God gives you a vision because it is always bigger than you. God will never give you anything to do that you don't need His help with. If it's bigger than you can do by yourself, then it must be a God-given vision, and you need His help.

Assess the strengths and weaknesses of making your decision this year or next year. How will the vision be funded? When will the idea be made public knowledge? How long will this vision live? Will it outlive you? Are other people helping you with the turn? Do these individuals have all of the information and resources? These are the essential questions to ask as you turn. If you don't give yourself time for proper assessment, your Titanic will sink because you miscalculated your success.

⇐ ◇ ⇒

*Most people move before they realize—
this has come to help and not to kill.
Don't let that person be you.*

Chapter Eleven

Don't Run for the New; Just Dig Deeper

"The voyage of discovery is not in seeking new landscapes, but in having new eyes."

-*Marcel Proust*

I was in Africa a few years back, and while I was there, I saw large mounds of what looked to me like a pile of dirt and dust. That's right. *Dirt and dust.* I didn't think this was an important part of Africa's landscape; that is, until my driver told me that these were gold mines.

The story goes that there was an African gentleman who took all of his money and bought the land that everyone else said was tapped out of gold. He chose to buy what others had thrown away. And since the land had already been used up, he was able to buy these tapped out mines for a fraction of the cost. The sellers of the land were anxious to make a sale, because they didn't think the buyer could do anything with what he purchased. They assumed that he would just use the land to fill it back up with dirt and make a subdivision of some sort. But what this young man decided to do with his new property, ended up changing the course of his life forever.

He called some miners back into work and asked them to dig deeper. A few hours later, they decided to keep digging. An extended period of time passed by, and instead of going home, they ventured beyond the normal levels of digging. Like a crazy man, he instructed the miners to continue. And when they got to what seemed like the bottom of world, they discovered more gold by digging past the regulated conditions and standardized norms! He found great riches because he believed there was something deeper.

Turning Point

The gold he discovered has presently made him a billionaire in Africa. In addition, his "digging deeper" philosophy has changed the course of action for informed miners everywhere. Now, mine owners all over the world are digging deeper because they are finding out that more wealth is somewhere far beyond what the naked eye can see.

As you turn toward your bright and brilliant future, don't run for the new; dig deeper. Your perception is not just about how far you can see, but how deep you can dig. Dig deeper into your resources. Dig deeper into your creativity. Dig deeper into prayer. You have no idea what lies beyond the normal levels of life. You've got to take a chance, follow God and go against the code. Yes, the code. Everything has a code. Everything has a barometer of normalcy. The code is what others use to define their customs and traditions. The code is what society deems as the regular way to obtain something. But when what you want is past the code, and when who you are doesn't fit within the code, you've got two options. You can either settle or you can dig. You can check-out of your future dreams and settle for the norm (which is the option small-minded people choose) or you can dig deeper by doing what no one else has done with the resources given them.

> *Your perception is not just about how far you can see, but how deep you can dig.*

Which will you choose?

Will you continue to keep up with the Jones' code, or will you create a new code?

I chose the latter a long time ago, and the woman Elijah met in Zarephath did, too. She knew the value of digging deeper. She found herself living during a desperate time in her life. In 1 Kings 17, the prophet approaches her and finds this poor woman outside gathering sticks. She has no more money left. She has no friends around. She has no husband to help her out. All of her gold mines have been used up. Her hope is completely gone. And

Don't Run for the New. Just Dig Deeper

in the lowest state in which this woman finds herself, Elijah doesn't wrap his arms around her in comfort. No! He tells her to bake him a cake.

Isn't it something how God will tell you to start your business on nothing more than a few sticks, a bin of flour and a jar of oil? The woman obeys the prophet because the prophet is sent by God. She digs deeper. She can't run to the local Wal-Mart to find new appliances to cook with. She can't run to a neighbor's house to ask for more sugar. She buys property on her prophetic word and she obeys Elijah's instructions.

He assures her, "The bin of flour shall not be used up, nor shall the jar of oil run dry, until the day the Lord sends rain on the earth." Sure enough, the word of the Lord does not fall to the ground. Her blessing comes from within her own home. All she had to do was learn how to think differently about what had become familiar to her. You should learn to do the same.

> *Maybe you've lost your creativity to see opportunities in the familiar. Maybe your struggle is keeping a zeal for the present gifts God has blessed you with.*

I know the temptation is to look for a new opportunity or move to a new location, because you think by moving or trying something different that your change of environment will bring prosperity. But, maybe you've lost your creativity to see opportunities in the familiar. Maybe your biggest struggle is keeping a zeal for the present gifts God has blessed you with. Maybe you're stuck on your own success and have forgotten about others around you.

The woman and the boy in the text are hungry and are about to die, but she feeds the prophet first. She puts down her agenda to provide for someone else.

Take a hint from the woman Elijah blessed. Before you look for success to reward you and you only, ask yourself, "How will my success help to feed others?" Dig deeper. Dig around you. Dig

———— Turning Point ————

beyond you. You never know the blessing God has in your barrel.

Before you jump to the newest idea, ask yourself: "Have I exhausted all options with what I have? Have I examined every corner of what I already possess? Am I using the creative mind God gave me or am I only satisfied with the code?" If you find yourself answering "no" to any of these questions, you already know what you need to do.

⬅◇➡
Dig deeper.

Chapter Twelve

Embrace Your Doubt

"Doubt is not the opposite of faith; it is one element of faith."
-Paul Tillich

Paul Tillich is a German-American theologian that I enjoy reading. Tillich said two powerful things that I think will help all of us in our turning point. First he said, "Decision is a risk rooted in the courage of being free." To this I completely agree. There is no better feeling than to make a decision that gives you the courage to be free—free from the expectations of family, or the pressures of buying a home just because everyone else has a home. There is no greater feeling than when you decide not to base your life on someone else's expectations. It is definitely a risk, but when a person decides that he or she is tired of where they are, then they have perceived a better place and they make a decision toward it. Doubt will be present and fear will exist, but the decision helps you to build courage enough to exercise that which you have declared.

> *Doubt will be present and fear will exist, but the decision helps you to build courage enough to exercise that which you have declared.*

The other quote that strikes me from Paul Tillich is this: "Doubt is not the opposite of faith; it is one element of faith." Which says to me that if a person is going to have faith, then doubt must be in the middle of it somewhere. Why? Because doubt creates the opposition necessary for you to succeed.

Everywhere in Scripture, we see doubt and faith holding hands with each other. Do you remember when Jesus comes off the mountain in Mark 9:24, and the man runs to Jesus because the disciples could not deliver his boy? Immediately Jesus asks, "Do you believe?" The man yells, "Yes I believe, but Lord help my unbelief." In this passage, doubt and faith are side by side. The man is expressing that he has doubt in the middle of his faith, but what is interesting is that God doesn't stop to deliver him from his doubt. Why does God allow doubt to come? Why does it seem like whenever you are going to step out on faith, that there is a little voice that says to you, "But what if it doesn't work?"

I believe God does not let doubt disappear because doubt and faith are both necessary to help you make the turn. What I mean is this: the moment you doubt him is also the moment you decide to believe him. I know it's crazy, but God is not trying to deliver you from the doubt. He's trying to deliver you *through* the doubt. So in a sense, whenever God is pushing you to have faith, he is also pushing you beyond the place you were in before faith took over.

> *...doubt and faith are both necessary to help you make the turn.*

You reached a point that you said, "I had to doubt him to believe him" and once you did, you were able to make the turn; you were able to free yourself from yourself; you were able to verifiably trust God again. If you had not doubted God, you would have never been able to recognize the moment that you believed.

It's like becoming wealthy. If there was never a point in which you can remember living paycheck to paycheck, then it's very possible that you will never fully appreciate what it means to be wealthy. A number of studies reveal that there is a high percentage of children from wealthy families who are spoiled by the wealth they did not generate. As a result, many of these inheritors end up making bad decisions and squander someone else's hard-earned money, all because they lack an appreciation for the process of acquiring wealth. Galatians 4:1-2 confirms in Scripture what statistics allude to. Scriptures says, "that the heir, as long as he is a child, differeth nothing from a servant, though he be lord of all; but is under tutors and governors until the time appointed of the father." In other words, until one endures proper training, he or she cannot carry the helm of the family. Training is important, and without it, your wealth will disappear quicker than a coin dropped in the middle of the ocean. I believe if more wealthy families would follow this principle, they would be more comfortable with the persons to whom they leave their financial trust. The last people we need to doubt, are our own family members; even though doubt is a part of my faith. Even though it is the element that God uses to strengthen my perception. Doubt can work in my favor (and not in my destruction) if I understand it as the thing that God allows into my business plan which challenges me to trust him and not myself.

Abraham knew how to embrace his doubts. Romans 4:18 says, "Who against hope believed in hope, that he might become the father of many nations, according to that which was spoken..." He had to go against the possible in order to believe the impossible. He had to focus on the words that were spoken and not on the son that God told him to sacrifice. If you begin to understand this, then you'll also understand why the greatest opposition of your life can become the greatest moment of opportunity in your life. It is the opposition you are dealing with that makes you more determined than ever. That is the moment when you decide to define yourself beyond your norm. That is the moment that you begin to perceive how big God is. That is the defining opportunity for you to declare to yourself, "I am greater than who I used to be," and you see how "the person I used to be would have never made the decision that I am going to make right now."

> *Change your way of thinking and embrace your doubts.*

CHAPTER THIRTEEN

The Blind Side of Perception
"The eye sees only what the mind is prepared to comprehend."
-Henri Bergson

Her name is Blanche Taylor Moore. Born in 1933 from Alamance County, North Carolina. She was a "P.K" (pastor's kid). Her father, P.D. Kiser, was an ordained Baptist minister who reportedly forced her into prostitution to pay for his gambling problem and alcohol addition. By the age of 19, Blanche had the highest paying job available to any female employee at Kroger. She was the head cashier, married with two children, and living the perfect country life. In 1971, her husband died and she began dating Raymond Reid. He was a manager at one of the stores where she worked.

She then met a preacher by the name of Rev. Dwight Moore—he was the new pastor of Carolina United Church of Christ. Within a year's time of her meeting Moore, her boyfriend, Raymond, took ill. Doctors say he had the shingles and it developed into what they call Guillain-Barre syndrome. He died on October 7, 1986.

But that was alright. By this time, Blanche had met Moore and in three years, they were married. April of 1989, they honeymooned in New Jersey, and upon return, Dwight collapsed after eating a pastry. The doctors began a toxicology screening to assess what could have affected him, but Blanche told the doctors that he had been working outside in the yard, and no one thought much of it. A week later, the results came back from the toxicology test.

Dwight Moore had twenty times the lethal dose of arsenic in his system; more than any living patient in hospital history at

Turning Point

that time. Miraculously, he survived this terrible season of his life but he never regained full sensation in his hands and feet.

This overdose of arsenic caused the State Bureau of Investigation to become suspicious. The Bureau decided to exhume all of the bodies connected to Blanche Moore: Moore's ex-boyfriend, Moore's ex husband, Moore's father, and Moore's mother-in-law. Arsenic was found in all of the bodies. And when they re-examined Reid's medical records, they discovered that his last dose of arsenic was fed to him while he was laying in the hospital bed!

Blanche was convicted of first-degree murder and was sentenced to die by lethal injection. She is prisoner #0288088 today. Twenty years later, she is fighting her death penalty sentence by appealing her case time and time again.

There is a blind side to perception that you must be aware of. Bad perception can open the door to deception. And when you are deceived, you give someone else authority to destroy your destiny.

> *Bad perception can open the door to deception… when you are deceived, you give someone else authority to destroy your destiny.*

Blanche Taylor Moore made a banana pudding that was to die for...literally. Every man she wanted, she used her pudding to terminate him; and she used her romance to destroy his perception. You must be aware of the blind side of perception. All perception is not good perception. If you allow yourself to be deceived by the people you trust, you may find yourself like one of Blanche Moore's husbands.

There is, however, a flipside to perception in the book of Judges that shines light on the positive ways in which blindsiding can work for someone's good. Ehud, the Bible reveals, was a Benjamite. All Benjamites were known for their dominant right-handed skill. Whenever they fought, they used their dominant hand to win. Well, Ehud was one of the few Benjamites who had a

The Blind Side of Perception

"weakness." He was left-handed. He was different. And God raised up this left-handed Benjamite in Judges 3:15 to deliver the Israelites from the captivity of King Eglon.

The story is an interesting one for many reasons. Ehud had to figure out a way to "blindside" the king so he could kill him (for the bondage under which he put Israel), but he also had a responsibility to bring the king a gift on behalf of the Israelites (which added to the increased taxation on Israel). In Judges 3:16, "Ehud made him a dagger which had two edges and he slid it under his raiment by his right thigh." By verse 17, we see that Ehud carries out the normal protocol and brings Eglon a present. But by verse 18-19, Ehud dismisses the other guys who accompanied him, and turns around to talk to the king in private. Apparently, Ehud was able to win Eglon's perception the first time they met because when he returns, Ehud tells the king that he has a secret errand to deliver. The king plays directly into Ehud's trap. Ehud takes out the dagger and kills the king, locks the door, and escapes before the blink of an eye.

> *The reality is, some people are attracted to your anointing, your gift, and your vision, and your talent; but they are not attracted to support it.*

Eglon let his guard down just like the preachers to whom Blanche Moore was attracted. One messenger murdered preachers. The other messenger saved them! The blindside of perception has a two-fold consequence. The reality is, some people are assigned to break barriers that have been built to keep you out of God's best. Others are attracted to your anointing, your gift, your vision, and your talent, but they are not attracted to support it; they are attracted to it so they can kill it.

A telltale sign for people like this are those territorial folks who have your back as long as you are with them. But, if they can't control you, then they threaten to kill your dreams. Or, if you decide to partner with someone else, then they try to devise a

———— Turning Point ————

plan to destroy your life forever. Perception can make you or break you, build you or destroy you. How you view a thing really does matter. And how you perceive a person will determine if you are going to conquer them or be conquered by them. Be very careful about your relationships with people. Someone who seems very sweet can also be very sour.

Pay attention to your blind side.

Chapter Fourteen

Believe Beyond Your Ability

"Blessed are they who see beautiful things in humble places, where other people see nothing."
-Camille Pissarro

All of us are on a journey toward something, but there are only three kinds of people that travel. There are pave roaders, dirt roaders, and woodsmen. Pave roaders are people who are only going to go where the road is paved. Which means, they are the type who always find confidence in going somewhere that somebody has already been. Dirt roaders, however, will leave the paved road to explore something else because they know that if they are going to do what is in them, then they can't do it like everyone else did it. Yet, dirt roaders still like to have structure, and they are prone to look for an easy route in order to accomplish their goal.

Then you have woodsmen. Woodsmen travelers are, in reality, visionaries. They cut trees down and make ways out of no way. They bring in their own asphalt. They build a foundation from the bottom up. They are hard working and unique. The world needs more woodsmen. The world needs more workers who will not simply rest on the laps of their forefathers and do nothing.

Which are you? Pave roader? Dirt roader or a woodsman?

You may be trying to figure out why your plan isn't working out right, but sometimes, the turn you've got to take is in the woods.

Benjamin Siegel, better known as "Bugsy," was a gangster, a killer and a dreamer. He was known for bribing cops, hijacking, pimping and...planting rose gardens. It's crazy, but Bugsy was the quintessential gangster with a dream. He wanted to one day own his own inn. And in the early 1900's when there was nothing in Las Vegas but a name and a desert, Bugsy built a hotel that has become an unofficial historic site in Nevada. The Flamingo Hotel has 100 rooms, a big pool, gourmet restaurants, a showroom, lounge, and of course, a casino. He literally built a palace in the middle of a desert. Today, it is remembered as the place where modern Las Vegas was invented.

Now here is where I get upset in all of this. Bugsy wasn't even a man of faith, and yet he had more faith than some of the Christians I preach to every Sunday.

When are you going to perceive what God has in store for you? When are you going to believe that God wants to use your idea to birth an invention that no one has ever seen? When are you going to finally walk away from the routine of normal living and move out beyond your ability?

If you don't believe beyond yourself, you will always feel trapped in regret and "what if."

I read an article titled "Positive Illusions about Talents Better," and in it, the writer says: "People with an exaggerated perception of their own abilities are most likely to succeed in life and at work...[I]f you convince yourself that you are capable, you will behave as if that were objectively true. Individuals who have a more realistic assessment of their abilities, tend to be more easily discouraged and are, therefore, less productive." What psychologist Shelley Taylor of UCLA figured out was this: when you focus on your inabilities, you are more likely to convince yourself out of it. But if you are convinced that you are capable, nothing can stop you. Taylor did not have a word for it, but our word is faith. She didn't understand the drive, the strength and the tenacity of spirit that God gives to believers, but we do. That is why we must believe

> *...if you convince yourself that you are capable, you will behave as if that were objectively true.*

Believe Beyond Your Ability

beyond our abilities. I know you thought that this entire section was talking about perception, but in actuality, it was really all about faith. You can't expect your vision to come into fruition without faith. You can't expect your seed to bring forth life until you water it with faith. Indeed the Scripture tell us that "faith without works is dead," but you also need to know that your works without faith will keep you wasting precious time.

Your work, your determination and your success need to be centered on the principle of faith—faith is the substance of things hoped for, and the evidence of things not seen (Hebrews 11:1). If you can see it, then you aren't perceiving the bigger yet. If you are copying off of someone else's invention, then you haven't tapped into your greatest dose of creativity yet. Believe beyond your ability. Have the faith to move away from the comfortable places. Build a business in a desert. You can do all things through Christ who strengthens you!

If you can believe it, then you can perceive it.

CHALLENGES

Chapter Fifteen

Accept Every Challenge

"You can't expect to meet the challenges of today with yesterday's tools and expect to be in business tomorrow."
-*Author Unknown*

Let's move away from perception and decisions for a moment, so that we can discuss the primary reason people stay stuck in the routine of every day life. Most people are afraid of the challenges they will face. Even the saints in the Bible were afraid to trust God and move out of their comfort zone; which is why "Do not be afraid" is found in the bible (in some variation) about 365 times. But know this: when you walk away from your job and return to school, you are going to face challenges. When you decide to apply for a promotion and you actually get the job, you are going to face challenges. If you buy a home or decide to get married and have children; none of these decisions come without their own levels (and sublevels) of challenge. At the same time, no challenge is too hard that your end result is not achievable. If God has given you the vision for it, then He's greater than the challenges that intimidate you.

> *If God has given you the vision for it, then He's greater than the challenges that intimidate you.*

So you have two options: stand at the fork in the road and never move forward; or, you can take the lessons you've learned from the decision and perception section, and apply them to the lessons you'll now receive about the challenges that every business, every relationship, and every ministry will face.

Challenge is not a negative word. The word 'challenge'

actually means a demand. So if you're challenging yourself, then you're putting a demand on yourself. If something is challenging you, then that means it is putting a demand on you.

If you look at challenges in this way, you'll be able to identify what is challenging you, and understand the purpose of those challenges. All challenges have a purpose. Is this in your life to make you a better person? Is it to make you a better Christian? Is God doing this to give you more patience or endurance? What is the purpose of the challenge? That is the first question you need to ask yourself. Then, you must realize that everything that happens in your life, when it comes to challenge, is designed to bring about a result. Everything that seems difficult is there so you can achieve better than what you can see right now.

Thus, when this challenge is over, you've got to ask yourself: Where is the benefit of this challenge? And if you are operating in the will of God, the benefit of every challenge will always yield a positive result. Now understand. The purpose of a challenge does not necessarily mean that the process won't have negative moments, but the benefit is always going to be a positive one.

> *The purpose of a challenge does not mean that the process won't have negative moments, but the benefit is always going to be a positive one.*

Let me give you an example of what I mean. If you are a minister or a caregiver, then I'm sure you know what it's like to visit the hospital from time to time. The more you visit the doctor for regular check-ups, the better the results will be; even if the doctor tells you something negative. You see, the purpose of that negative diagnosis is to bring about a positive. The doctor assesses your situation so that he can tell you, "This is what you are doing correctly and this is what you are doing incorrectly." There is an assessment made, and that assessment helps you to identify the problem, so that you can fix what will only get worse if you don't assess it.

Accept Every Challenge

Most of us will try to avoid the doctor and self-diagnose or self-medicate the problem. But if you try to self-medicate, then you're going to end up with the wrong results. You can't do half of what the doctor says and then get upset if the prescription doesn't work.

I say all of this to say, you have to embrace the fact that challenges are a part of the prescription. Challenges are going to be a regular part of your progress. If they aren't, you have ceased to progress. Ever wonder why your man loves video games or football? It's because of the challenge. Ever stopped to figure out why she loves going to the gym even though, in your mind, she's in really good shape? It's because of the challenge. All of us need them, and most of us pretend like we don't want them; but without challenges, our lives would be boring. Don't ever underestimate a good challenge. Challenges are literally the life of us. There is something about us that doesn't feel like we're living unless we have a good challenge. Why? Because the area where you are most challenged will always become the area that God grants you the greatest victory.

Now, accepting a challenge does not mean to go out and make unwise decisions. I'll never forget the time I was taken on a house tour by a real estate agent. The home was worth $17 million dollars. *It was a really nice house.* I felt like "Hey! I could really get used to this!" Especially when I walked into the bathroom of the master's suite. There was a mirror-like double fireplace in the bedroom and bathroom, and a retractable plasma TV near the Jacuzzi that was controlled by a remote. It was a serious home! Elevators, staircases, acres...you name it! I could imagine myself in it. I informed the agent that I liked the house and the agent introduced me and my mother to the owners. We had a very good conversation, we talked about the home and they really seemed to like us. But when they told me the price, I chuckled and said to my mother, "this must be somebody else's house!"

So we left the home and the agent told the owners that while I loved the house, it was more than I could afford. A few weeks later, I got a phone call from the real estate agent. She had spoken to the owners and they said that they really liked me and wanted me to have this home. The agent was excited because she was about to tell me some unbelievable news. I was full of anticipation.

"What is it?" I asked.

She said, "They are dropping the price for you!"

"Really?" I asked.

"Yes! Yes! Yes!" she screamed. She could hardly keep her composure when she said, "They are going to reduce the price by 14 million dollars and give you the home for 3 million!"

Now to some people, that was certainly God moving in a miraculous way for me to get that house. But the truth is, I still could not afford the house even with the unbelievable reduction. The point I'm trying to make is this: there are some things that will seem to be God but they are not. God will never tell you to do something that will keep you in bondage. I'm going to prove it in Scripture. If you read Proverbs 10:22, you will discover these words: "The blessing of the Lord, it maketh rich, and he addeth no sorrow with it." The key to this scripture is the second half. The Lord does make rich, yes, but if there is sorrow attached to your money, it is not from God. God would never tell you to buy a property that will keep you bound. He just won't do it. Don't just jump into things "just because." Examine your options. Be realistic. It makes no sense to purchase a house you can only afford to live in for the first thirty days.

Choose the challenge. Accept every challenge. Choose wise challenges.

CHAPTER SIXTEEN

Anything Not Challenged Will Remain Permanent

"The manager accepts the status quo; the leader challenges it."
-Warren G. Bennis

The norm is the code. We all know the norm because we know what the book says. We know the norm because we know what the law says. But when your vision is taking you outside of the normal boundaries, you've got to reach into yourself to figure out what your new permanent place will look like. You were not designed to be kept within boundaries. You were not created to be enslaved to another man's success story. The day you find freedom will be the day you declare, "My norm is not your success." That is when you are free to challenge every permanent boundary around you.

My father went to jail at one point in his life. The reason he went to jail is because he was subpoenaed to speak against one of his church members who had disclosed confidential information to him as their pastor. The judge told my father that protestant ministers were under obligation to tell the court system whatever their members told them in private. Catholic ministers, however, were not held to that same legal mandate. Catholics were free to maintain confidentiality in court because the law said it was O.K. to do so. And so, my father said: "I'm not testifying." And he didn't. As a result, they put him in jail for contempt of court.

The case caused such an uproar that it ended up in the Supreme Court; and they overturned it. He changed the law for every Protestant minister all because he decided not to bow down to the norm. What I'm saying is this: the law remains permanent until it is challenged. Your situation will remain the same until you get fed up enough to do something about it. Anything that is not challenged in your life will remain permanent in your life. If you don't challenge your children, they'll always settle for the passing grade. If you don't challenge your employees, they will never have the tools to start their own company. If you don't challenge your church, they will always look to you for all of the answers. If you don't challenge yourself, you will end up stuck in the legal system of law and normalcy.

The reason that Jesus is so controversial is because He never allowed the law to remain permanent. He challenged the law. Jesus says to us in Matthew 10:34 "Think not that I am come to send peace on earth: I came not to send peace, but a sword. In this verse (and the verses following), Jesus deals with traditional mindset that someone has called norm, versus having a new understanding of your reality, and deciding not to settle for the status quo. In others words, Jesus came to turn the law upside down and change the world while still honoring what the law told him to do. The law said that healing couldn't happen on the Sabbath (Luke 14:16). Jesus challenged this by asking the Pharisees, "If one of you has a son or an ox that falls into a well on the Sabbath day, will you not immediately pull him out? And they had nothing to say."

> *You have to get fed up with your laws. See yourself bigger than your borders.*

Jesus knew how to leave his accusers speechless. He challenged the law until something changed. The law also ordered a woman caught in the act of adultery to be stoned to death. But Jesus challenged that law by asking the onlookers, "He that is without sin among you, let him first cast a stone at her" (John 8:7). I know you may feel as if you can't do anything about your limitations, but the truth is, you can! You have to get fed up with your "laws" that limit your progress. See yourself bigger than your borders. When you get fed up with the law that was not designed

Anything Not Challenged Will Remain Permanent

for you, that is the moment that you turn.

Michael Jordan. Who knew his name before Carolina gave him a chance? Michael Jackson—out of the norm. Larry Bird. Simon Cowell. Selena. Oprah. Michelle Obama—and the list goes on and on, especially as we move forward in time. We are beginning to see and learn new names. These names are figures that have found success because they were committed to going out of the norm. I'm certainly not the only person who watches the Grammy's and asks, "Who are they?" "Where did they come from?" But you know what, I don't need to know them. Someone else does. In fact, millions of people know that particular person because that musician developed a target audience.

Challenge yourself to expand your target audience. Challenge yourself to build your own underground railroad.

Roadblocks are only detours; they do not stop you from getting to your destination.

> *Move out of your permanent comfort zone. Challenge your law. Challenge your norms.*

Bill Gates. Who knew his name thirty years ago? No one. But he decided one day to step out of the norm. He decided to challenge his laws. Now what's interesting about Bill Gates is this: he was not supposed to have the opportunity. He was not supposed to become a billionaire. He dropped out of Harvard to pursue his passion, and while in Seattle, a company by the name of IBM approached Gates because they needed an operating system for their new hardware. The software they needed would transform an expensive paperweight into something that would perform everyday needs like word-processing. Gates did not have what they asked for. He did not have the system. But he told them, "Come back tomorrow," and when they left, Gates went out and bought the Intel operating system for $50,000 outright. He sold it to IBM for $80,000 and did not stop there. He also secured the license rights so he would not

Turning Point

end up binding himself to IBM's law. He made sure that he would be able to sell this license to other manufacturers as well.

Move out of your permanent comfort zone. Challenge the law. Challenge your norms. Challenge your neighborhood. Even if you don't have the resources, ask God for the wisdom and instruction you need to make your vision come to pass.

The United States has had laws for as long as it was established, but people fought those laws until new boundaries were created. There is no more segregation because someone challenged the law. Interracial marriage is legal because someone challenged the law. The only thing in life that will remain permanent is the thing that is not challenged.

>
> *You're the next greatest challenger of everything normal around you.*

Chapter Seventeen

Raise Your Standard

"Each of us will one day be judged by our standard of life –not by our standard of living; by our means of giving—not by our measure of wealth; by our simple goodness—not by our seeming greatness."
-William Arthur Ward

Some time ago, one of the guys from my church asked me an interesting question about restaurants. He wanted to know why some restaurants make it and others don't. Immediately, the word that came to my mind was: standard. It's really all about the way someone sets a standard for themselves, their visions, or their family, that determines how long it will last.

Then I reminisced a bit to a time when I visited Beijing. While there, I remember searching forever to find an English-speaking channel. Once I finally found it, it didn't really matter what I was watching. I just needed to view something that I could understand. Well, there happened to be a television special on that featured some of the best restaurants in the world. It drew my attention immediately because some of these restaurants were well known and others were quite exclusive.

The one that I remember most vividly, however, boasted seven figures annually and they only served 8 people per day. In addition, the restaurant was booked one year in advance already!

I thought to myself, "How in the world could someone pull off owning one restaurant—not a chain; just one restaurant—and be able to serve 8 people per day and still pay the bills?" Then, the cameras revealed the inside of the eatery. If you saw some of the exquisite detail in this place, you knew for a fact that they weren't serving Happy Meals at this restaurant. No, no, this was a five-diamond restaurant that I hope I can afford to visit one day.

─── Turning Point ───

The difference was the standard. A business will last forever if they maintain a high standard. A marriage will outlive years if the standard of commitment is higher than the emotion of love. What is your standard? What are you unwilling to compromise for your dream? You may think you are excellent, but what are you comparing yourself to? If you think you have an excellent prayer life but you compare yourself to someone who doesn't pray, then maybe you need to get around people who can challenge you to be better. If you think you can sing, cook, act, or play sports, make sure that your evalutators are equally as good as you are. Otherwise, you are just feeding your ego with a dose of unhealthy affirmation.

The only way you will succeed in making this turn is if you decide not to live on local standards. God has called you beyond the local scene. And by expanding your landscape, you are also able to ask, "What is my standard in comparison to the world, and not just the little city street I live on; or the local church I go to?"

> *The only way you will succeed in making this turn is if you decide not to live on local standards alone.*

Standards are everything. If you are single and you desire to be married, realize that a person sees you by the advertisement you wear. If you have a high standard for yourself, you won't give your heart to the first man whistling. You won't even respond to a whistle. *Employees*, you can't continue blaming your employer for not giving you a promotion if you aren't coming to work on time. Your standards must translate into everything you do. The reason Michael Jackson is known as the best entertainer that ever lived is because he spent millions of dollars on music videos when other musicians were spending thousands. His concerts were so out-of-the-box that everyone ran to hear him because they never knew what they were going to get. But the reason Michael's standard was set so high, is because he valued himself.

Another key component to raising your standard is

understanding who you are and who you are not. Our tendency is to become too familiar with people, places, and things that are "beneath" our standard of living, and in the end, we end up devaluing the gift within us. We have ten things that we are good at doing, and instead of maximizing on one talent, we try to multi-task ourselves into doing everything.

What is your purpose? How do you find it? I will tell you. In order to find your purpose, you must know your value. The place where you are valued the most, is the place where your purpose can be best fulfilled.

In Luke 4, Jesus experienced what some of us might call a "devaluing" of sorts. He visits the synagogue in Nazareth (the place where he was raised), and begins to read the Word of the Lord to the "churchfolks" gathered there: *"The Spirit of the Lord is upon me, because he hath anointed me to preach the gospel to the poor; he hath sent me to heal the brokenhearted, to preach deliverance to the captives, and recovering of sight to the blind..."* In a few words, Jesus exposes who he is. He is reading Himself. He is the WORD. He is the incarnate one. God is reading about God, and the people miss it. They do not understand his value. Instead, they whisper, "isn't that Joseph's son?" The same is probably happening to you. Instead of people recognizing who you are, they try to control your purpose. They only allow your gifts and talents to be used for *their* platform. They aren't inclined to recognize anything greater in you than they see in themselves.

If this is happening to you, do not continue to let unqualified people appraise your worth. It's time to raise your standard and know your value. If you do not, you will only reach one small level of success, because you were too afraid to step out of the prison of familiarity that others put you in.

Challenge yourself by raising your standard.

Chapter Eighteen

Reaching Unity

"Coming together is a beginning. Keeping together is progress. Working together is success."
-Henry Ford

When 9/11 happened and terrorists attacked our country, America actually became the United States of America. For just a few months, political parties were not fussing about left wing politics or right wing politics. Everyone focused on helping one another, giving love, and showing support. Communities everywhere were more concerned about protecting their country rather than protesting against it. American flags flew high and the words "God Bless America" were written across every bumper sticker, window and teleprompter.

It's a shame that a nation who boasts unity in the name of its country, cannot come together until tragedy. But the truth is, America is no different than the church divisions we see and allow every Sunday. And yet, God works through our mistakes and teaches us more about Him as we go through life. This is the true beauty behind being a Christian, and the best thing about reading the Bible: you can learn from people's mistakes.

In Genesis 10:8-10 we find an interesting situation going on. A people come together in Babel to do a certain thing; and at the end of the story, God does not like what they are trying to do. So, God interferes. But, what we rarely pay attention to is the fact that God has no problem with their process. God honors his principles even when we turn left and lose focus. The principles don't change. This is why there are many billionaires in the world who don't serve God. If someone learns how to work the principles, then they can find true success. Anyone can be successful;

Turning Point

Christians just have no excuse. We know where the success comes from and we have insight into the kingdom of God that others do not have.

So in this text, we see a bad ending but the story is built on the principles of unity. It is, in fact, one of the best examples of unity that has ever been written in Scripture. First of all, there is a man by the name of Nimrod who became quite popular in the earth. Nimrod was a hunter before the Lord and before people (Gen. 10: 8-9). Nimrod was a special man. He was not just a community changer. He was a world changer. He wasn't just a church reformer. He was an international leader. He was a hunter by trade, and so that meant that he knew how to chase. He knew how to go after what he wanted, and as a hunter, he chased his prey until he captured it.

Is your success important enough for you to chase after it, even when you don't feel up to it? I know you may not "feel God," but the question I want to know is: are you chasing God? What are you chasing after? Because whatever you chase, will eventually affect you and your future. If you never chase, you won't get lunch. If you never chase the challenge, you will never reach your vision. It will only be a visual to you. But when you begin to chase after your vision and embrace the responsibility that comes along with it, now you are chasing.

> *If you never chase the challenge, you will never reach your vision.*

Let me tell you something about a hunter. I am an expert—I hunted for a little over two days—so I can tell you a few things about hunting. A hunter's attitude is one of determination and perseverance. They will go out and work if they feel like it or not. A hunter does not waste his time looking for something to shoot. A hunter, instead, studies the seasons. He knows the right time to go where and he doesn't try to find something when he knows it is not the right season.

All of this skill was what made Nimrod so popular during

his day. And before he knew it, Nimrod had become so powerful that he was able to mobilize an entire world into building a tower that had never been built. Genesis 11:1 says, "and the whole earth was of one language, and of one speech." This means they were of one mind and one mouth. They spoke the same language even though there were many different dialects. They understood one another so well, and respected Nimrod so much that when he said move, all of the people in the world got up and "journeyed from the east," and dwelt in the land of Shinar (Genesis 11:2). Can you believe this kind of unity?

The people following Nimrod were not like many of us who can't work with anyone. *You know the kind.* They will never be unified to anything because they are so caught up in being unique. They want to be noticed. They've got to be seen. But if you really want to succeed in life, you've got to challenge yourself to be unified with a vision. Commit yourself to covenant with someone. No one lives on a one-man island. You're going to need someone to help you carry out your dream eventually.

> *...if you really want to succeed in life, you've got to challenge yourself to be unified with a vision.*

The story goes on in Genesis 11:2 and the people are so unified that they decide, "Let us build a city and a tower whose top may reach unto heaven." The Lord comes down to see the city in verse 5, and the reason the Lord must come down is because everyone in the world is participating in the vision. Everyone is likeminded. Everyone is unified. So much so, that Genesis 11:6 says, "And the Lord said, Behold the people **is** one, and they have all one language." The word "is" implies a singular unity. The people are so unified that they are not an ARE; they are an IS. When one speaks, all of them speak.

Even though God was displeased with their end, God was impressed by their unity. The people in Genesis model for us the challenge of unity; and still we are struggling in our marriages, in our churches, and in our business partnerships to *be* one. Can you imagine the strength of anything that is united? Can you imagine a choir singing in robes without having that one alto standing up in black? Can you imagine what it would be like if the two really became one flesh in marriage? Just imagine. Just visualize what it might be like to work together in unity and in spirit. Your business would be better. Your team would be better. City councils would be better. Government would be better. Schools would be better. The possibilities are unlimited of what could be better if we could just do one thing: UNIFY.

Reach for unity. The challenge is great, but the reward is greater!

CHAPTER NINETEEN

The Problem with Procrastination
"Procrastination is the grave in which opportunity is buried."
-*Author Unknown*

Once upon a time, there was a man who struggled with procrastination. Everything he set out to do, he didn't do it when he said he would. He'd never turn things in on time. He always put off work until the last minute. And he complained all day because he was still single, still lonely, and still unaccomplished.

The guy walks into a dinner. He's late, of course, but he comes into the cocktail area and stands across the room alone. He sees a woman; she's very beautiful. She's the woman of his dreams—everything that he would've hoped for.

He's not the kind of person to move too soon, so he says, "I'll talk to her in five minutes." Five minutes turn into fifty.

The woman sees him but does not say anything to him. She isn't the kind of woman to *ever* make the first move. She has etiquette, she has "standards" and she thinks to herself, "Well, if he likes me, he'll come over here and greet me. If not, I'll just enjoy some music and go home."

The dinner party ends and the guy goes home without ever meeting her. He runs to his desk to finish his work. He'll be up all night writing a paper that was due last week. But that's O.K. He's so used to his condition that he doesn't even realize how slothful he has become.

The phone rings.

A friend of his calls and tells him how nice a certain woman is that he met at this cocktail party. Mr. Procrastinator realizes—this was the same woman that he had seen from across the room. He becomes angry. He screams inwardly at his friend for taking her away from him. But the only person he could become angry with, was himself.

This is a hypothetical fairy tale, of course, but the principle still stands. Procrastination is a success killer. It will drown your vision before the water fills up the swimming pool. If you let procrastination set in, you won't feel the pain of being in neutral but you will become drowsy. You develop into a nonchalant person who eventually gives up on the dream God has put inside of you. I cannot tell you how many people have missed their turning point before, simply because they were not willing to crawl out of the ditch of procrastination. Now, God has brought the opportunity back to you again, and you are still afraid to walk across the room and go after what God has designed for you to enjoy.

> *Procrastination will drown your vision before the water fills up the swimming pool.*

Where does procrastination come from?
Where is the root of the issue?

The real reason people procrastinate is because they have over thought the process. Ever met someone who just thinks too much about everything? They think about budgets that aren't real. They calculate money that hasn't come in yet. They are just addicted to thinking. As a result, they are so challenged by their own over-thinking that they begin to fear success more than they embrace it. They think about success and they dream about being balanced and content, but all of a sudden, like the shy boy in the ballroom, they become afraid and "comfortable." They are comfortable with how things are; comfortable with the excuses they've made up. And when they realize that life is quickly passing them by, they become bitter toward people who are excelling beyond them; simply because they haven't done anything significant lately, assuming they have plenty of time left.

The only way to conquer procrastination is to get up and do something. If you bake the cake and you mess up the recipe, keep on baking until something starts tasting right. Get up and apply for a job, even if the economy says we are in a recession. Doing something is certainly better than pretending to do something. Sometimes the job will come to you by networking with people, and not by the ordinary application process. Whether you like it or not, the vision that God has designed will come to pass.

If you read Habakkuk 2:2, it will motivate you to do something quick! The prophet says, "The Lord answered me and said, write the vision, and make it plain upon tables, that he may run that readeth it. For the vision is yet for an appointed time, but at the end it shall speak, and not lie." The Scripture never says that *you* need to speak. In fact, the Scripture does not even say that you need to be present for the vision to speak. The vision will speak with or without you. It shall speak, even if you aren't there to speak for it. The business will go on with or without you. The Broadway show will find another actor. That beautiful woman or handsome man will one day find love; with you or without you. It will speak! So why let *it* speak for you when you have the anointing to speak for it?

The challenge you have to conquer is your fear. Move out of your comfort zone and change your friends if you must. Don't allow procrastination to steal more of your time and talent. The enemy loves it when we bury our talents and forsake our God-given purpose. Be passionate enough about your vision not to let anyone else speak in place of you!

Don't miss your chance! The vision will speak with you or without you.

Chapter Twenty

The Real GIANT is Your Vision

"Don't wait until everything is just right. It will never be perfect. There will always be **challenges**, obstacles and less than perfect conditions. So what? Get started now. With each step you take, you will grow stronger and stronger, more and more skilled, more and more self-confident and more and more successful."
-Mark Victor Hansen

They say big things come in small packages. Well, in 1998, this saying was proven. One of the most unexpected automobile buyouts happened. Volkswagen acquired Rolls-Royce & Bentley Motor Cars. The little *Beetle* bought the giant *Rolls*. No one imagined that it could happen, but it did. In 2003, BMW reclaimed the rights to Rolls-Royce, but those five years in which Volkswagen owned Rolls-Royce should be an encouragement to every small business owner who dreams of one day being listed in a *Fortune500* magazine.

The real challenge, as this story proves, is not with the giant. The real giant is your vision. No matter how tall or short, young or old, you can do whatever God put in you to do. The giant that you see is your problem, perhaps, but the invisible giant that the giant doesn't see, is his problem. You need vision to take on a giant. You need vision in order to look eye to eye with someone bigger than you or a company name more famous than you, and still, trust God for the open door.

> *No matter how tall or short, young or old, you can do whatever God put in you to do.*

I'll never forget working out with my M.M.A (mixed martial arts trainer) and my security staff. I was the smallest guy

Turning Point

in the room and during one exercise, my trainer told me to flip over my security guard. Now I believe God, and I have the power to speak to mountains, but that this didn't seem like it was going to work. Why? Because my security guy is a BIG guy! Nevertheless, I decided to try.

I prepared myself by bending down—thinking that I flip him over on my back, and just before I grabbed him to throw him over, my trainer stopped me and said: "Williams, you can't think about strength! Think about technique."

> *The more capable you see yourself, the better you will be able to relay your competence.*

The key is this: He walked me through a technique that allowed me to flip over every guy in the room. I was the *Beetle*, but I was able to conquer the Rolls.

The way to ensure that you will succeed is not by your physical strength; it's by your spiritual vision (your technique). If you pay attention, God will introduce people to you who can assist you in carrying out the vision. All you really need is the right viewpoint, and the boldness it takes to face your giant. The more capable you see yourself, the better you will be able to relay your competence. You think you're too young, but let me tell you about a guy named Cameron Johnson. He started his first business at the age of nine. He designed greeting cards, invitations and stationary. In a year, he put $50,000 in savings and invested the money into the email forwarding company called My EZ Mail; and that investment generated over $3000 per month in advertising revenue alone. At the age of fifteen, Cameron was receiving checks between $300,000 and $400,000 per month. And before graduating high school, his assets were worth over $1 million (not including his salary). He's presently 23 years old, and he's traveling around the world to promote his latest book titled, *You Call the Shots*.

Maybe you think you're too old. Well, there is woman by the name of Ann Nixon Cooper. No one knew her name nationally until Obama ran for President. She made national news during his victory speech and she was apart of every major political triumph; all because she let her vote speak for her. She was 106.

Another young man, Harry Bernsten, authored his first book *The Invisible Wall* at the age of 96 in 2007.

What is your excuse? What are you afraid of again? You are David; and the truth is, Goliath is afraid of you. Not because you are huge in stature, but because you are huge in vision. There is nothing that God puts in your path that is unconquerable. It may be big, but it is conquerable. It may be intimidating, but you can certainly conquer it.

I love David because he was not afraid of Goliath. We know this because in 1 Samuel 17, David talks junk to his giant and calls Goliath out: "You uncircumcised Philistine." *Now, David! Was that necessary?* We already know that he is a Philistine but by the mere fact that David calls him uncircumcised, we understand that these are fighting words. David is not moved by the list of skills and warriors that Goliath has conquered. Even though this wrestling match is like Buster Douglas fighting Mike Tyson, David is not moved. His confidence is not in himself. His confidence was in his God. And though Goliath was bigger than David, the truth is, David's God was bigger than Goliath.

When you lose faith in yourself, turn around and look in your corner. Something is always in your corner that is bigger than your problem. Your God is bigger. Your vision is better. Your aim is precise. You can't miss the mark! Why not? Because the giant is so big, the rock is bound to hit him somewhere.

The real giant is your vision. Goliath, watch out!
Get to work!

Chapter Twenty-One

Challenged to Be Content

"I am not saying this because I am in any need, for I have learned to be content in whatever situation I am in."
-Philippians 4:11

No two human beings are the same. There is only one true Mona Lisa painting. Anything else is a copy. Yet, so many people are living their lives trying to be copies of each other. For what? Why would you want to dress like him or sing like her? The Human race is not a robot of people who look alike, act alike, or sound alike. All of us are different. We come from various backgrounds and some of our stories are so crazy that nobody would ever believe it. That's what makes YOU, YOU. You have no business trying to copy your success with mine. You have no time to waste learning how to mimick someone else's strategies for success. You are fearfully and wonderfully made, the Bible says. You are special in the eyes of God. How dare you allow somebody, anybody, to disqualify you from success all because in their minds, you don't meet their standard? Who made them God? Who made them your source?

> *If you're going to make a turn, you've got to be confident in yourself. Challenge yourself to be confident in yourself.*

If you're going to make the turn, you've got to be confident in yourself. Challenge yourself to be confident in yourself. Know what God wants you to have and be satisfied with that. Quit envying other people's stuff. Quit kissing the ground other people walk on. What God has for you is for you. Don't go after anything that doesn't match with God's architectural design for your life.

Turning Point

Just go after God, and God will bring success to you. Yes you—with your educated or uneducated self; or you, with your proper or country self; or you—with your knowing how to dress or needing help with coordination self. Go after God, and God will bring success to you.

You don't have to worry about "looking the part." The part looks like you. The missing piece has your name on it. Everything you need to succeed and prosper is already within your reach.

The third richest man in the world, Warren Buffett, still lives in a 6,000 square foot, five bedroom home that he bought in 1958. He's a billionaire today, but he lives in a home that cost him and his family $31,500. You would think he would own yachts and cars and homes in every country, simply because of the level of success he has attained, but no two people are exactly the same. Buffet is disciplined and focused. Buffet is a planner. He doesn't just think for the present. He thinks for the future.

When asked about his secret to success, Warren Buffet said, "If you don't feel comfortable owning something for 10 years, don't own it for 10 minutes." His home has everything he needs to survive and he's happy with himself. In the same way, you've got to learn to be happy with yourself, no matter how much money you have in the bank or how much property you own. Be content in your own skin. Find joy in what God blesses you with, and resist from envying what other people have. Covetousness doesn't look good on anyone. Envy will destroy your creativity. And the truth of the matter is, everyone will not be a millionaire. You've got to know that. You must accept that to some extent. If everyone who reads this section on challenges walks away thinking, "I'm going to be the next Oprah; I've just got to challenge myself," you have the missed the point altogether. What if Oprah really needs to be the next YOU!? Know who God made you to be, figure out what God had in His mind for you to achieve, and run after those goals with all tenacity and perseverance.

Apostle Paul never became a millionaire. In fact, life was better for him (in some people's minds) before he found Christ, not after. After surrendering to God, he was given a mission that would change the world and change the church forever. Paul was imprisoned for the sake of Christ, he was persecuted, but had Paul not been comfortable in who he was, we wouldn't have half of the New Testament today. Paul was accustomed to luxury. He had already experienced loss. He was an educated man and he was a man that was always thinking about the next move. Still, Paul said, "I have learned in whatsoever state I am in, therewith to be content."

Now don't get it twisted. Contentment does not mean complacent. Contentment does not give you a pass to be lazy. Contentment simply challenges you to control and curb the lust of your mind. Contentment helps you to establish some clear-cut limits. It helps you to stop coveting what other people around you have.

As you make the turn, become challenged by what you see, but content with what you have. Maximize off of every opportunity God sends your way. Stay in your lane. Even if you become a billionaire, don't buy land or waste money on things just because you want to project an image of success. Your success is not for you alone. It is for the up-building of God's kingdom. Start a scholarship fund. Become an entrepreneur. Take a family vacation. You don't have to wear your money everywhere you go.

Know what God wants you to have and be satisfied with that.

Reinvent Yourself

Chapter Twenty-Two

Reinventing You

"... as we enjoy great advantages from the inventions of others, we should be glad of an opportunity to serve others by any invention of ours; and this we should do freely and generously."
-Benjamin Franklin

I believe one of the highest personal tragedies of life is when you find yourself living in your own skin but you can't find YOU. That is a horrible place to be. It's a horrible ditch to dig yourself out of. To live in your own skin and can't find you. Many people suffer from it, most are in denial about it, and as a result, they will never succeed in life because of it. Which is why you'll notice that I have chosen "Reaching in me to find me" as this book's subtitle. I know it sounds a bit puzzling to grasp at first, but the truth is, every key to success lies within you. You've got to reach in you to find you. Your greatest goods are not outsourced from others or imported from another country—they all reside in you. You are the key that God uses to unlock good fortune, but if you are not careful, you can become the door that is keeping yourself locked out of it. You are the mastermind behind the prosperity plan God has designed for you, but if you are not deliberate about turning, you will become the partition that is constantly getting in the way of your own prosperity. Reaching in you to find you is crucial to your success because no one else will ever have more influence in your life than you. No one's opinion will ever trump yours. No one's vote will ever matter more than yours. You can turn and you can triumph if you just

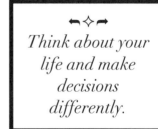

Think about your life and make decisions differently.

Turning Point

take the time to search for the treasure in you.

This searching process, however, is no easy task. It's no walk in the park. It is initiated when you change your way of thinking, and good thinking will help you to change your way of living. The way you think determines how you live. And the way you live influences how much you can give. But it all starts in your mind. The lab of success is your mind.

Benjamin Franklin knew this. As one of the founding fathers of the United States, Franklin failed hundred of times before introducing that one famous theory concerning electricity. Forward-thinking kept him focused on success. His past gave him every reason not to succeed. He had no right to achieve anything great. His was one of poverty and non-privilege. He was the youngest of seventeen children. His daddy, Josiah, was a candle maker. And when he died, they wrote the words "without an estate or any gainful employment" on his tombstone. How humiliating. How embarrassing. Franklin was exposed to all of this, but he didn't let his father's story become his own. He decided to reinvent himself. He decided to make up his own rules. Even though Franklin failed arithmetic in grade school, he didn't let a grade determine his aptitude. And when people asked him about his failures, Franklin would say, "I didn't fail the test, I just found 100 ways to do it wrong." His mindset was his greatest tool.

> *An invention does not mean you will not invest precious time working on an idea that doesn't lift off the ground.*

This is the way you need to look at your present condition, as well. An invention does not mean you will not invest precious time working on an idea that doesn't lift off the ground. Most of your ideas will never be known by others. But with every method you choose and with every theory you explore, your mind is always being exercised. The lab materials are constantly being mixed and remixed to make the best living invention the world has ever known. If you keep this in mind, your mistakes will make for a good victory party when that one idea jumps off of the pages and becomes a tangible prize.

Don't waste your creativity copying off of someone else's ideas. An invention is a new, fresh-off-the-press discovery that you come up with and sample in the hopes that it will change someone's perspective on life. Start this wheel of fortune by re-inventing you. See yourself differently. See the world differently. Think about your life and make decisions differently. What about your children? What about your family name? Will anyone know you ever existed after you depart from this life?

Re-invent you by changing your mindset. Benjamin Franklin started with a theory. This theory started in his thoughts. And his thoughts were enhanced the more he used his mind to rework that theory. Noah did the same in Genesis 6. He was told to build an ark for a flood that the world had never seen before. He invented something by letting his thoughts coincide with God's divine instructions. God is not going to leave you empty-handed or empty minded. He'll provide the measurements for the ark if you will change your thinking about the storm.

You've got an invention in you that has never been imagined before. You have ideas that are waiting to be birthed. There are everyday opportunities presented to you, but if you aren't thinking the right way, and if you are not wise enough to pay attention to the signs, you will bypass them. You will lose sight of what matters most. There must be a psychological transition. Your thinking changes your environment for you. Your vision of success must not only be embraced, but it must live in your thoughts; so that everyday you're walking in what you're thinking. Every day your theories can become the beginning stages of your new reality.

⇐✧⇒

Re-invent You. Reach in YOU to find You.

Chapter Twenty-Three

Study Your Audience!

"Study your audience more than you study your lines...or you will lose your audience."
-Kevin Williams

At 15 years of age, I was living the life. I was popular in school, I was popular in church, and best of all, I had me a little girlfriend. She was a cute lil' girl who liked me a lot. I liked her a little, but she could never know how much I thought about her. Well, one day, my girlfriend and me got into a heated argument. It ended in tears (hers of course) and pain. I remember snapping at her, "I'm finished with you! You don't know what you got, girl! You don't know who I *is*." Mind you, I was 15! I was just getting into this dating thing and I knew my value enough to know that she wasn't doing what she needed to do. So we broke up. It was a Wednesday. The next time I saw her, it was Sunday morning. The scene was unforgettable. She came to church and had on lipstick, new earrings and a new dress. She was looking g-o-o-d and she knew it! To top it off, the guys in the church had heard about us breaking up, so to them, she was fair game.

I couldn't wait until church was over. During the entire service, while people were screaming "Amen," I was sitting on those drums thinking about what I would do when I got over to her. Because my daddy was a preacher, I knew the perfect words with which to begin the conversation. I stomped over to her pew, and with one eyebrow lifted, I sternly whispered, "The devil got into this relationship! Since we are victorious, we can't let the devil defeat us. We need to work this thing out!" Of course, we would reunite and a month later, she would do something that would make me break up with her again; and just when I thought

Turning Point

I was finally done, she would come to church with a new getup and hairdo. I would go back to her like a devoted pet goes back to his owner, and the vicious cycle would go on and on and on.

What was she doing every time she realized I no longer wanted her? She was reinventing herself. She had studied me enough to know that I would always come back as long as she was able to take me by surprise. No matter how threatening my words were and no matter how convincing my bark was, this young lady knew how to get what she wanted.

Do you? Do you know how to impress the boss that fired you? Do you know how to make your spouse "walk" (not fall) back in love with you? Do you fall under the category of people who lose what they love simply because they got used to what they had? Or are you like my ex-girlfriend—the kind of person who is smart enough to discern when a situation is getting dry and spice it up before it's too late.

As you re-invent yourself, know that your invention is not only for yourself, but for the audience you intend to impact. Study your audience more than you study your lines. Study your audience more than you study your résumé. Preachers who only prepare a sermon by reading a few Scriptures are missing the crux of what it means to engage a congregation. You must study your audience or you will lose your audience.

> *Study your audience more than you study your lines [or] resume... or you will lose your audience.*

Safe to say, she wasn't the only one who mastered this technique. Sean "Puffy" Combs and Oprah Winfrey are two of the wealthiest Black entrepreneurs alive—and I believe that most of their wealth is attributed to the fact that they knew how to reinvent themselves. Sean John Combs changed his brand more times than Elizabeth Taylor married! At least five times—from Sean Combs to Puff Daddy to P. Diddy to Sean John, and now to Diddy. He is a *true* businessman with a clothing line, two restaurants, a movie production company, a music label, and he is

Study Your Audience!

the producer of MTV's *Making the Band*. Combs is multi-dimensional and he didn't want his rapping audience to associate every business decision to his hip-hop identity. So, he was always reinventing himself.

View life in the same way. If you are going to be about kingdom business, you cannot allow your gifts to be buried inside of the church walls. You can speak in tongues in church, and that is fine, but when you are trying to sell property or purchase property, tongues will just have to wait! There is a greater network base waiting to know your name, and you've got to be bold enough to step outside of the comfortable space you call church, or home, or work, or wherever you hide. Get out of the box! Change your name! Reinvent yourself.

Oprah's talk show would have been an "I remember when" talk show if she hadn't decided to re-invent herself. It began as nothing more than another tabloid talk show. It mimicked a Phil Donahue, Wendy Williams, or a Jerry Springer. It lacked substance but it entertained—temporarily. By the mid-1990s, however, Oprah decided to reinvent her show by focusing more on literature, spirituality, and self-improvement. It wasn't the popular thing to do at the time, but it ended up changing the way hosts moderate talk shows forever! Now she has a book club, a top-of-the-line magazine, and she's producing more shows than any entertainer alive. Ten years after her re-invention, she was hailed as one of America's first black billionaires. Thankfully, those statistics have changed and there are far more African-American billionaires now than ever before, but Oprah was a trailblazer in every sense of the word.

When are you going to influence people beyond your comfortable reach? When will the big shift take place for you? David realized in Psalm 37:25 "I was young and now I am old." *Look around*. The world is getting older by the minute. You're not the same person you were ten years ago. Adjust your life so that it matches the person and plan you desire to invent.

How do I begin reinventing myself after I have studied

―――― Turning Point ――――

my audience? Simple. To re-invent yourself, one needs a fresh idea from an old plan. One needs to move toward the future by carrying history forward. If you're trying to introduce your vision to a new audience of people, then you have to hang around different people. You can't get upset when you attract what you advertise. Change things about the way you are perceived on the outside, so that people can feel comfortable with what you present to them. Remember, you attract what you advertise; and you confirm what you respond to.

Anyone who is serious about making the turn, will make a change. Change your speech—professionals won't take you seriously if you are always cursing and joking. Change your attitude—your future love won't appreciate how condescending your voice is whenever you're speaking to your mother on the phone. Re-invent yourself the way Paul did. He didn't continue operating with a Saul mentality after he was converted. Instead, he took something away from his lesson on the road to Damascus and realized that, "in order for people to gain respect for me, I've got to show it better than I can say it." God changed his name, but maybe you need to change yours. You aren't defeated or destroyed. You are destiny-driven. You are one step away from your greatest decision. You are one phone call away from supporting your family for the rest of your life. Your name is not weak. You are a winner. You are the strongest person alive. At one point, you may have allowed misuse to mess up your self-perception. But this is a new day. You're on the verge of the greatest chapter of your life, and God is getting ready to turn the page.

What has your name changed to? What do your loved ones call you? Most importantly, how do you view yourself?

Chapter Twenty-Four

Fear Ain't Always a Bad Thing!

"Many of us crucify ourselves between two thieves –regret for the past and fear of the future."
-*Fulton Oursler*

Visions are like babies—they hurt birthing them and they hurt raising them; but they'll give you joy in the end. There is a tension, then, between what I love and what I must endure. There is a war going on between what I desire to achieve and what I fear I will not achieve. Reinventing yourself means that you are not afraid of fear. To reinvent you, you must be honest with you about you. If you are afraid of success, name it. If you are fearful of fortune, admit it. The same way visionaries need a little bit of doubt mixed in with their faith, you also need a bit of fear mixed in with your faith. When fear and faith collide, it births passion. When passion manifests, it brings perpetual purpose.

> *When fear and faith collide, it births passion... [and] passion manifests... perpetual purpose.*

Now let me pause right now and admit: I can already predict some "deep church person's" response to the title of this chapter. Just pray for me. I am really challenged by deep people in church. And the reason they challenge me is because they will quote Scriptures without thinking about the reality of their situation. The deep response would be, "God has not given us the spirit of fear,"—yeah, yeah, yeah—but let a dog start chasing you in the middle of the street. You better have some fear within you or you're going to get bit. You can say what you want about not having any fear, but let a tiger jump out of the cage at the zoo! If all you do is quote 2 Timothy 1:7, I guarantee you: someone will be either hospitalized or buried.

Fear ain't always a bad thing. Fear is a necessary signal in our human anatomy that helps us to decipher between a good choice and a bad choice. Fear is an alarm clock that will always wake you up and try to convince you to do something, and do something quickly.

I will never forget watching a television program that featured mothers who were badly injured but quick responders. They would rescue their children from the danger of an unexpected accident before their senses caught up to the reality of the situation. One woman, for instance, literally flipped an entire car over with her bare hands to prevent her baby from dying beneath the car. In this case, her passion was centered around her child. But her fear was centered on the possibility that her child would not make it out alive. Together, these two opposing forces caused this regular-sized woman to do the unthinkable. Flipping a car over? How many women (or men for that matter) do you see doing something like this on a daily basis?

> *When you stop being so deep and allow yourself to redefine your fear, you may unlock certain powers that you didn't know you had.*

This is precisely the point I wish to raise. When you stop being so deep and allow yourself to redefine your fear, you may unlock certain powers that you didn't know you had. To operate in fear is unhealthy; to have fear and appropriate it toward something else, is beneficial. The best dreams come into fruition all because someone mixed passion and fear together. Peter was afraid to walk on the water but he was so passionate about getting to Jesus, that he went against his human limitations. Many people criticize Peter for sinking, but when Peter stepped out of that boat, he taught us to bring fear with us as we move out in faith. Criticizers of Peter also forget to ask the question: "How did Peter get back into the boat?" I surmise that Peter used his feet to get there; which means, even though he fell before, he learned to conquer his fear later. What makes you any different? Bring your fear with you. Bring every reason you shouldn't do it with you as you decide to do it. Bring the naysayers who don't want you to succeed beyond their level of success—bring them with you. Bring your non-qualifications with you. Bring your not-so-good transcript with you. God loves to help those who have every reason to turn around, but still they pursue beyond their doubts and fears.

You might be the only person in your family to think the way you do, but the more you fear, the more ammunition you have to change what you fear. The closer you get to the fire, the farther you walk away from the demon of idleness. Fear isn't always a bad thing. Every Christian needs a good bit of fear and reverence within them so that they do not take God for granted. Fear communicates my love for God. My fear helps me to rearrange my faith. Fearing the future puts me in a class all by myself. If there was nothing to fear, then I am not growing or learning anything new. I am never being challenged. Everything around me is comfortable. No person around me is sharpening me to be better than I was last year. I am going nowhere and challenging no one.

Thank God Supreme Justice Sonya Sotomayor brought her fear with her to Princeton University, and later to Yale Law School. She graduated valedictorian of her high school class, but Princeton was an entirely new adventure. In her first year she realized how difficult it would be to assimilate into an Ivy League Institution. Not to mention, there were only 30 Latino students (even fewer of them were women) studying at Princeton while she was there. She admitted her fear and took the necessary steps to conquer it. In the summer months after her first year, friends would find Sotomayor in the library studying all day. She would read beyond the assignments given and she would frequently attend writing tutorials to improve her writing.

Justice Sotomayor graduated from Princeton *Summa Cum*

Laude in 1976. Her last two years there, she received all A's. Her fear was in her lack, but her passion was in the law. Had she given into her fears and not challenged herself, she would have never become the Court's 111th justice, the first Hispanic justice, and the third female justice.

>
> *God has not given you the spirit of fear – I agree. But learn how to reinvent your "fear" so that God's glory can be seen through your passion.*

Chapter Twenty-Five

Find Your "Good Place"

"I don't care how poor a man is; if he has family, he's rich."
-Dan Wilcox and Thad Mumford

You're in a house and everyone in the house is crazy. You don't have enough money to leave the house. You don't have enough money to buy another house. So what do you do? You reinvent your surroundings and transfer to a different place. Find another room, turn off the lights, put on a candle and add a little soft music so that you can get a different aroma going for yourself. Find your good place. Your good place is the God place. Your good place changes the temperature from conflict to resolution. Your senses need to know that something has changed. Your body needs to realize that you are in control of it and not the other way around. Tune out everything and shift to that good place so that everything around you will follow suit even though you haven't left your environment physically.

> *Your good place changes the temperature from conflict to resolution.*

As people with busy schedules, two or three full time jobs or energetic children, you must find time to turn down the volume and focus. There must be time in your daily routine just for you and God to spend together. This particular type of reinvention does not require money or a time share. Those are very nice if you have them, but with them or without them, all you really need is a mental shift. Always be aware of the fact that you live in three dimensions: a physical dimension, a mental dimension and a spiritual dimension. The physical is the least important but the mental and spiritual are of primary importance. When the weight gets heavy, you will find yourself needing to get away from it all; but what happens when you can't leave the house you've built? What happens when the job you want to let go of, doesn't want to let go of you? What happens when the spouse you want to leave needs you to be their strength? What happens if you're in prison (of any kind)? You most certainly cannot leave physically but you can leave mentally and spiritually. And if you master this technique, you'll get out of prison five years before your body ever got out.

How?

Well for starters, you can begin by reinventing the way you think—it's the only way to stay sane when everything else is insane. In Judges 11:3, we find these words: "Then Jephthah fled from his brothers, and lived in the land of Tob: and there were gathered vain men to Jephthah, and they went out with him." Now here is a little Bible Exegesis 101. The words *Tob* means "a good land" or "a good place." Jephthah escaped from his homeland to this "good place" because his family had been fighting him incessantly. From early on in his childhood, Jephthah survived unfair treatment. He was guilty by association. Scripture reveals in Judges 11:1 that his mother was a harlot, which means she was not married to Gilead (Jephthah's father), but Gilead was certainly married to another woman! This, of course, created tension in the household. The kids would pick on Jephthah and eventually, they kicked him out and denied him the right to receive any of his fathers inheritance. Not because of anything he had done wrong. Simply because he was a "son of a strange woman" (Judges 11:3).

What does one do when they must reinvent themselves because of someone else's wrongdoings? How does one begin to patch up the holes of another person's problem? Well, the first thing you must do is realize that you aren't the only one living in the situation you're in. If you've ever been accused of something that wasn't your fault, you have inherited Jephthah's dilemma. If

Find Your "Good Place"

your family has ever mistreated you over something you had no control over, then Jephthah and Kevin Williams are in your corner. We've been where you are.

Jephthah's testimony gives a bit of relief to those who feel as if they are the so-called "black sheep" of the family. We want to get away and disappear, and unlike some of us, Jephthah gets kicked out. The good news is, the "good place" was the God place. While Jephthah was living in Tob, he was able to perfect his art of war and he was gaining popularity by the day. Many "vain men" came to him (Judges 11:3) for help. Now, this word vain simply means that these men were without resources. They were broke, busted, and disgusted; but they drew to Jephthah because they saw something different in him. They saw something in Jephthah to which they could relate.

You may not want to read this, but the truth is, people see something different in you. You're trying to figure out why there is so much chaos going on around you, but most times it is because of the influence you have on other people. Let me say it differently. People seem to draw to you and you don't do anything to draw them. People tend to call you to listen to their issues or to seek your counsel, and you don't have an advanced degree in family, parental, or psychological counseling. You have something within you that makes even the vainest man believe. You have a good place that makes others feel good about themselves. Do not push people away! Bring them to your good place. The good place right now may be your vision. Learn how to mentally and spiritually transfer yourself to the place where God is taking you. Don't transfer yourself to where you've been. Don't worry over things you can't change. Don't blame your half-brothers for calling your mama a harlot. Just transfer yourself over the folly, and focus on the future. Go to the place where God is most pleased. You may never see it now, but someone is watching you and waiting on you to help them see things better.

The reason I love this story is because a few verses later, war breaks out against Israel; and the very ones who pushed

Jephthah away, are coming back asking him to help deliver them from the children of Ammon. To put it plainly, what goes around comes around. Judges 11:6 says, "and [the elders of Gilead] said unto Jephthah, Come, and be our captain, that we may fight with the children of Ammon." Come and be our captain? Are you serious? The very ones who were fighting me as a child, want me to use these same fists to fight off someone else?

The bigger picture is this: family fights prepare you for real fights. Your family can become your best shield and your hardest competition. If you can convince your family, you can convince anybody. If you can stand after your big brother has tried to beat you up, you can stand against the worst of them.

Remember, in every temptation, God has provided a way of escape. Sometimes you have to escape out of a certain place within your mind. Sometimes you must leave the surroundings and imagine something greater--something bigger. The best place to go is your future. Thinking about your future should always be the playground of your spirit. Why? Because your body will always end up where your spirit and mind stay the most.

Go to the good place. Shift your way of thinking. The cross becomes bearable when you're thinking about the place beyond the tomb.

CHAPTER TWENTY-SIX

Who are Your Influences?

"Bondage is – subjection to external influences and internal negative thoughts and attitudes."
-W. Clement Stone

In the previous chapter, we discussed how to reinvent yourself even if something happened to you that wasn't your fault. But what happens if something *is* your fault? What happens when you make a bad decision and now, everyone has a negative impression of you due to something you caused? This chapter will look into how to reinvent yourself from a mistake you knowingly and admittedly committed.

Monica Lewinski is known around the world as the woman who participated in one of the largest political scandals in our country. At the time she wasn't married. She was only 22 years old. And the repercussions of this mistake have affected her life in ways that I'm sure she wishes she could change. If the topic of the scandal comes up in conversation today, fewer people even remember a lady by the name of Linda Tripp. She was Monica's "influence." In 1996, after Lewinsky was relocated to a new job in The Pentagon, she confided in this co-worker, Linda Tripp, about the affair. She, of course, wasn't aware of the fact that Linda Tripp began recording her conversations with Lewinski. When everything surfaced, Tripp had over 20 hours of recorded evidence that Lewinski never knew about! Everything Tripp said, Lewinski obeyed. Tripp advised her to save gifts. Tripp told her to keep the "blue dress" as evidence. They were friends. Tripp was her

---

"Washington: Court Victory for Linda Tripp." *National Briefing.* New York Times, 4 Nov. 2003. http://www.nytimes.com/2003/11/04/us/national-briefing-washington-court-victory-for-linda-tripp.html?ref=linda_r_tripp. 3 Sep. 2010.

influence. But when Lewinsky was given an opportunity to give final words at the grand jury trial, she told the jury, "I hate Linda Tripp."

These final words suggest to me that she never wanted it to go there in the first place. You must be careful about allowing certain influences to alter your life. If you are not, influences can drag you straight to hell.

Luke 8:26-35 tells of a man who met Jesus in the country. This man had devils in him for a long time and he slept in the tombs. The man said his name was "Legion: because many devils were entered into him," but what is interesting is that this man had been influenced by outside sources. He has been affected by certain things he had been connected to. We all must be careful with what we choose to connect ourselves to. Sometimes we can connect to an outside source and it can affect us in a way that makes us act completely abnormal. An easy indication of someone who is affected by an outside source is when you have to ask them, "Why are you dressed like that? Why are you talking like that?" They are acting abnormal and they don't even realize it themselves.

> *...be careful about allowing certain influences to alter you life.*

In the text, the man is running around without any clothes. Surely he has been influenced by someone else. This is not his nature. If you read this story in Matthew 8:28, however, you will discover a missing link from the Luke text. Matthew 8:28 reveals "and when [Jesus] was come to the other side into the country of the Gergesenes, there met him two possessed with devils, coming out of the tombs..." Wait a minute. First there was one. Now there are two. What happened to the one man who was with Legion? I'll tell you what happened. I believe the man stayed long enough to impart his spirits into the other man. He hung around the other man long enough for Legion to take on his abnormal ways and behaviors.

Who are Your Influences?

You have to be careful what influences you allow to come into your life. Before you know it, you will end up like Monica Lewinsky: recorded, reported, and left alone—doing something you never intended to do.

Another famous woman who ended up in a far worse situation than this, used to go by the name Selena. Many of us knew her. She was the talented Mexican-American singer who was so gifted, that she had begun to unify the Americas with other Spanish-speaking countries through her music. Her influence transcended her singing ability. When Selena opened her mouth, the whole world dreamed with her. But her downfall occurred when she decided that she no longer needed her manager's services. Yolanda Saldivar was the founder of Selena's fan club and she managed Selena's boutique. There was very little about Selena that this woman did not know. When they suspected that Saldivar had been embezzling Selena's money, the two engaged in a heated conversation. It ended in Saldivar shooting Selena in the back; and Selena died not many hours later.

The question is: who are your influences? If someone is sharing their influences with you, they could also be sharing their demons. Be careful. The man in Luke had a major situation here. The Bible tells us that this man had these devils for a long time. He was naked, he wouldn't go home, and he was hanging around past things.

Are you hanging around things that should have expired in your life? Do you find yourself constantly going back to the tomb areas that have long been buried? Maybe you are not the "thing" that keeps causing you to go back; maybe your influences are encouraging you to go back.

How does one reinvent himself or herself from allowing influences to control him or her? Well, Scripture says that when

---

Hinojosa, Cassandra. "Born to be a Star: Selena known for her humility." *Caller-Times*. Corpus Christi Caller Times. 31 Mar. 2005, http://www.caller.com/news/2005/mar/31/born-be-star/. 3 Sep. 2010.

the demons are called out, an immediate shift occurs. Truthfully, Jesus is the only solution to your demonic problem. As the demons are being called out, the man fights what is in him in order to get better. If you're going to re-invent yourself, you've got to fight what's in you. Don't settle for the stigma. Don't live life as a Legion. Don't allow your flesh to control you. Ask yourself, "What's leading me to do these things that I have no business doing?" Then fight it until you can't fight it anymore.

 Here's the good news. When the demons come out of the man in Matthew 8:32, the Bible says that they depart into a herd of swine and the swine perish in the waters. Luke 8:35 tells the rest of the story. When the people "went out to see what was done," they came to Jesus and found the man, "sitting at the feet of Jesus, clothed and in his right mind: and they were afraid." What happened in this text? Quite simple. When the man was rid of his influences, he was reinvented by Jesus. The demonic influence had come to persuade this man into committing suicide. This is why the pigs end up drowning in the sea. But the man is freed by Jesus and immediately we find him sitting—which means he wants to learn; he is clothed—which means he wants to change his image; and he is in his right mind. This means he has shifted from what people have made him, to what God has created him to be.

After you reinvent yourself and do away with the influences, prepare for people to be afraid of where you are going. The people became afraid of him because he shifted and reinvented himself. If you ever reinvent yourself to be what God has called you to be, you'll make people terrified of your future. You'll intimidate people simply because you have the ability to prove to any individual how possible it is to change even after something you caused. Remember: just because you caused it, doesn't mean you're dead.

 Chapter Twenty-Seven

Never Let Anyone Gamble with Your Future

"He who advises you to be reserved to your friends wishes to betray you without witnesses."
-Don J. Manuel

"Coming to America" is one of the funniest movies of all time. This 1988 American comedy about an African prince who comes to the United States to find a woman to marry, has been seen by millions. The star, Eddie Murphy, is credited for writing the film and many of his famous lines have been quoted over cookouts, family gatherings, and comedy shows everywhere. Financial reports reveal that this movie brought in $288 million in revenue! But in 1990, another report revealed that Murphy had stolen this movie from a man named Art Buchwald.

Buchwald v. Paramount was a civil suit alleging that the film's idea was stolen from a 1982 script. Paramount viewed the script but did not accept it. And, despite the many false claims and excuses, Art Buchwald ended up winning the case. Indeed, someone had stolen his script, profited monetarily from it, and forgot to pay him. Their excuse was that after marketing the film and producing it, the movie did not make enough to pay the original writer. They showed accounting records and marketing costs as an attempt to silence Buchwald and keep everything under the radar. Before the lawsuit was over, however, Buchwald won the breach of contract and the court ordered Paramount to repay him the monetary damages. They decided to settle the case out-of-court but the fact of the matter is, someone was busted.

As you reinvent yourself, you must not be ignorant. There are many people out there who want to steal your genius ideas

Turning Point

from you. Never allow anyone to gamble with your future. Protect your dream, protect your image, and protect your vision. A visionary who tells his or her dream to everyone is asking for disappointment. Sometimes you must learn the art of silence. Keep your vision to yourself until you have procured the rights and the protection you need to safeguard your ideas. If you do not, you will end up like Buchwald, suing a monumental production company like Paramount over ideas that were yours from the beginning!

> *A visionary who tells his or her dream to everyone is asking for disappointment. Sometimes you must learn the art of silence.*

Joseph had this very problem: whenever he received a new dream, he would tell his brothers. Whenever a new idea would come to mind, he would spill the information into the laps of those who later devised to do away with his life. Genesis 37:4-5 says "And when his brethren saw that their father loved him more than all his brethren, they hated him, and could not speak peaceably unto him. And Joseph dreamed a dream, and he told it to his brethren: and they hated him yet the more."

Now here is the problem I have with Joseph. Joseph should've already known to keep quiet when he saw that his brothers wouldn't speak peaceably to him. There are always signs before destruction, but sometimes we walk right into the door of destruction because we ignored the floor-mat of warning signs. Joseph continues to confide in people whom he knows do not like him. He is ignorantly giving away his script to Paramount Productions, and the next time we see him, he's being thrown into a pit—by his brothers!

There are jealous people around you. Deal with it! Face the truth, and be free from the delusion. If you are doing anything significant in life, jealous folks will hover themselves around and attempt to make you fall at any cost. But the greatest revenge is success. The greatest comeback is a promotion. You don't have to

Never Let Anyone Gamble with Your Future

bow down to your enemies; let the Lord handle them. In the meantime, you just keep working on your vision.

A person who has reinvented himself has also reconstructed his friends. He knows the persons in whom to confide and he knows who to keep at an arms length. Bishop Jakes once said, "there are three kinds of people you will meet: confidants, constituents, and comrades." You may only have one true confidant in all of your years. Confidents are those who will tell you the truth and rejoice when you succeed. Confidants care about YOU more than they care about your success. If you are up, they are there. If you are down, they are there. If you end up with two or three confidants, you have struck gold!

Then there are constituents who only come in your life as subjects of your vision. They participate and they assist, but to them, it is nothing more than a business transaction. The same is true for the comrades. They are only in your life temporarily, but they serve their purpose and then they depart. If you're going to ensure that your vision gets handled properly, never put your trust in the hands of a constituent or a comrade. They will steal your ideas now and then charge you for them later!

> *When you reinvent yourself, you make a decision to redefine your friends. Always be aware of the possibility that someone may try to steal your plan and ruin your future.*

When you reinvent yourself, you make a decision to redefine your friends. Always be aware of the possibility that someone may try to steal your plan and ruin your future. Don't be paranoid but be prepared.

Keep in mind all of your opponents. Watch how people react to you when you come to them with good news. Jesus tells us to "pray for our enemies and bless them that curse you." By that He doesn't mean to bless them with the opportunity to destroy your destiny. He actually means to bless them by deciding not to divulge any information to them that you wouldn't share with a stranger.

Do not allow anyone—family, friends, or close relationships—to gamble with your future.

Chapter Twenty-Eight

Nothing is Ever Simple

"We have learnt that nothing is simple and rational except what we ourselves have invented; that God thinks in terms neither of Euclid nor of Riemann; that science has "explained" nothing; that the more we know the more fantastic the world becomes and the profounder the surrounding darkness."
-Aldous Huxley

Some time ago, I knew a young man whose father pastors a very large church. He came to me and said something quite strange.

"I want you to teach me how to preach," he whispered.

I whispered back, "Why would you come to me when your father is a pastor whom I admire?"

He shot back his response with certainty, "I want you to teach me because my father would only teach me how to preach like him. I don't want to preach like him."

To this I responded, "Well if I teach you anything, I'm certainly *not* going to teach you how to preach like me. If I did, then I would rob you of YOU."

Immediately, he started glowing like an anxious child. He asked, "So what would you teach me?"

I replied, "At your father's permission, the first thing I would teach you is my purpose in your life. I am what they call stain."

He asked what I meant.

My response was this: "My responsibility is not to make you into panel, it is to stain the wood that you already are so your natural grain comes forth. If I do that, then you can't be duplicated and no one will ever be able to accuse you of being a copy of me." From there I went on to give him a few lessons.

> *In order for you to impact people, you'll have to reinvent them based upon what life has thrown at them.*

Lesson #1
Treat people like they are unique and important. Whenever you preach to others, you must see each situation as an original and not a duplicate. Circumstances are different and people are different. In order for you to impact people, you'll have to reinvent them based upon what life has thrown at them.

Lesson #2
Maintain integrity. Your integrity will open more doors than your invention will. Your integrity moves people to want to work with you. The greater the integrity, the greater the value of your vision.

Lessons #3
If you want to change people, make sure to change yourself. Change yourself by challenging yourself. Set high expectations, but at the same time, don't think that you have arrived after you have reached a certain goal. Go above what you have accomplished. Go above what your parents have accomplished.

Lesson#4
Never underestimate the people who can help you. Many times, we meet people in our lives whom we think serve no real

purpose at all. Then we find ourselves in a foreign country or on a new job, wishing that we could speak to the very person we threw away. If you value people, you build purpose. You can't build purpose without people.

I shared these lessons with him and I'm sharing them with you because I do not want you to walk away from this section thinking like me. I was sent in your life, perhaps, to develop your thoughts. But you are reading this book so that you can reinvent this book; so that you can mix this information with your own creativity and make an impact on the world in a way that no one else can. You may try to duplicate what I say or do, but the truth is, it's not that easy. Nothing is ever simple. Duplicates only become reminders of the original. Your best work will never be taken seriously because people will associate you to what you look like.

This is what Jesus tried to tell the disciples when he said in John 14:12, "he that believeth on me, the works that I do shall he do also; and greater works than these shall he do; because I go unto my Father." He was basically saying to them: DO YOU! Go above what you have seen me do. Raise the standard. Dream bigger than your forefathers dreamed. See the world healthier than it is right now; see the country more economically stable than it is right now. See your family happier than they are right now. See your church growing exponentially all because you are there, and not just because you followed a few steps toward success.

If you only follow my blueprint, my recommendation, and my words, then you are nothing more than a robot recapitulating my mode of action. You are too great to be subsumed by someone else's ideas. You have too much leadership within you to follow someone who should be working for you! Don't shy away from the difficult days. If God knew that you were not fit for the job, He would've hired someone else.

As you reinvent you, make sure not to compare yourself to other people's notion of triumph. The easy way is not always the best way. The simple way is sometimes the most boring way. If you are going to make the turn, embrace the challenge. If you want to reinvent yourself, then "walk into love" (don't fall into it) with a new perspective on life. You will not be able to escape the process. A process is a chain of events or shifts in seasons. If you are willing to endure the hard times of the project, you will see increase on your promise.

Now What?

 Chapter Twenty-Nine

Be True to Your Commitment

"Commitment unlocks the doors of imagination, allows vision, and gives us the "right stuff" to turn our dreams into reality."
-*James Womack*

Congratulations! You have made the turn, and you are fully equipped to go after the vision. But now what? What do you do to maintain the vision? What do you do after you have faced your fears, defeated Goliath, made good decisions and reinvented yourself?

This section will provide a few answers to the question, "Now What?" The first thing that you need to remember is this: never forget the purpose of your vision. Never. The purpose of the vision is the original intent of why something was given to you in the first place. Never forget why God blessed you with a business or a spouse or a new plan. If the vision loses its purpose, it has lost its life. If you forget why God blessed you, you will find yourself in the pit all over again.

> *Visions can only survive off of their original intent.*

Visions can only survive off of their original intent. So one way to remind yourself of your purpose is to answer these questions: "Why are you doing what you are doing? Who is the vision for? What was the original plan?"

If your vision is designed to help particular people, then focus on why you are doing it and not the benefit from it. Anything connected to the kingdom should never be for self-service anyway; it should be for the purposes of serving God and serving God's people.

Turning Point

The second thing you must consider is the maintenance of your vision. Just like you purchase a new car or a new house, the issues will not arise while the leather is still fresh and the carpet is still clean. The problem with many successful people is that they cannot maintain their success because they lose the integrity of that success. The dream cheapens. The goals are undermined. They achieve it, and instead of maintaining it, they want to dismiss this vision and go after something else. But maintenance is more important than the achievement or the prize. If a person is body building, they have to maintain a diet, and they must eat what body builders call "clean." They eat clean, they exercise clean, and they live clean. But what happens after the competition is over, is what will happen to you if you aren't careful. Some body builders go back to eating the same way that they used to eat, and then their bodies don't maintain the fitness that they had during the competition; all because they lost the integrity of their commitment.

> *If [success] is going to be sustained, then you must continue to challenge yourself and continue to progress, in order to succeed.*

This is not just applicable to men and women who lift weights. How many "lose weight quick" sponsors are seen on the cover of magazines after losing tons of weight; and then all of a sudden, a year passes by and many of them lose their motivation all because they stopped receiving financial endorsements.

Success in business or in ministry is no different. If it is going to be sustained, then you must continue to challenge yourself and continue to progress in order to succeed.

Remember you will always have challenges every step of the way, so as you progress, your immediate questions for assessment should be: What is my greatest challenge now? How am I expanding the original intent of this vision now? Your challenge won't be fearing that somebody will pass you. It does

Be True to Your Commitment

not matter how quickly others are moving in relationship to your motion. Your vision is not their vision. Your only challenge should be a desire to continue to progress past where you seemed to have plateaued. It is so easy to slip into cruise control, but you can't let that happen. Without progression, there is decline. In order to maintain, you've got to progress.

I will not forget when my father took me to see this movie when I was a little boy. And at the time, there was nothing like this movie I saw. The movie was called "Star Wars" and in the movie, there were flying battleships and strange looking creatures. As you watched, you literally felt like you were flying with them. Back then, no movie was greater than "Star Wars." But now that I am in my forties, I have looked at the very same movie and realized, "this doesn't seem to have the same effect on me that it did when I first saw it." And so now, I am challenged by the fact that the movie has not changed, but I have changed. I have matured and I have progressed. And the subtle reality is this: you cannot continue to be wowed in your present by the things that used to wow you in the past. You must maintain that level of appreciation for your past, but move forward and take on new dimensions of perception, decision, challenges and reinvention.

>
> *Don't change up now. Be true to your commitment.*

Chapter Thirty

Be Self Motivated

"When a man asks himself what is meant by action, he proves that he isn't a man of action. Action is a lack of balance. In order to act you must be somewhat insane. A reasonably sensible man is satisfied with thinking."
-James Baldwin

You are your greatest fan. No one can celebrate you better than you. This is the next lesson you need to remember after you make the turn. Motivate yourself by figuring out ways to keep yourself excited about the vision. When you first get the vision or attain some level of success, you will automatically become excited. It's a new thing going on in your life. But when you are working the vision, you can fall into the trap of losing your steam and exhausting your excitement. So write down your vision or chronicle the process that you went through to get to where you are, and you will always have something to re-excite you later on. Every visionary needs something that will bring him or her to the level of momentum they need to keep going.

> *Drive yourself from within and not from without…To be driven from within is the greatest gift that anyone can have.*

Drive yourself from within and not from without. Learn to be happy by yourself and with yourself, even if others are happy for you as well. To be driven from within is the greatest gift that anyone can have. To be focused on what you have to do is more important than anything else. Motivation's automobile is run by the motor of focus. You can tell if you are focused on something when you resolve, "this is not just a want; this is a must." And signs of this mindset are evidenced in your determination, drive, and desire. Other people will go home after work, and you will still be there practicing what is not even required for you to know. You will burn the midnight oil in your studies, even though you are a B student on average. When you get motivated to succeed in your vision, then a B is no longer enough. You want the highest and you want the best because you realize that excellence lies within you. You tap into this level of motivation when you are actually doing what you were created in this world to do. And because you are God's best candidate to carry this out, no one else will ever be able to outshine you!

> *You want the highest and you want the best because you realize that excellence lies within you.*

Here are three more tips for motivating yourself.

1) Motivate yourself with the humble understanding that you are the best, but it is only because you work hard at it. Any singer worth their salt will make singing look easy, even though they have had to work on their breathing, warm up scales, and trouble spots. A gift is not something that you do effortlessly. It is only the grace that you do it in that allows it to seem effortless.

2) Realize that motivation is always driven by a force of fear or faith. I remember a few years back, I had a friend who complained that his leg was hurting, and he was limping. He said it was very difficult for him to move it. He had not gone to the doctor yet but concluded that it might be a sprain. I told him that he needed to walk in order to stretch it at least. So we decided to walk, but we proceeded to walk very, very slowly. All of a sudden, we hear a dog barking. And the barks get closer....and closer; and sooner than we realized it, this large dog was coming our way!

I immediately went into protection mode because I knew my friend was hurting. But when I turned to my right to tell him that I was there to cover him, he was already down the street! Fear motivated him. The bark was the only noise he needed to forget about his pain, his limp, and even his poor friend.

3) Have benchmarks in your life that help you to track your growth. Benchmarks become key for you to identify when you are successful and when you are not. By producing benchmarks, you learn how to assess your own success and pace yourself. What are benchmarks? How do they function?

Benchmarks are like tabs on a ruler that help you to measure your arrival and destination point. If you break down a vision with benchmarks, you might say something like this: a vision has goals. Goals have beginnings. And to everything you begin, you assign a certain amount of tasks to it. Everything has to work together and everything that works well, needs to be tracked and archived. If you motivate yourself, then, by keeping track of your benchmarks—whether great or small, successful or unsuccessful—then you don't get lost in the struggle of the day because you are frustrated that something didn't go your way. You must know where you are going and create a time pattern of what you have accomplished. Even the greatest men and women get discouraged when they can't remember what they've accomplished. Don't allow your dream to die that easily. The pressure of the immediate thought can make you feel like a failure—until you look at your benchmarks.

Thus, motivate yourself. Realize that you are greater and stronger than your present challenges reveal. Then, encourage yourself to become the invincible person that you really are.

Chapter Thirty-One

Be a Progressive Visionary

"Stay committed to your decisions, but stay flexible in your approach."
-Tom Robbins

One of the most difficult components to any vision, strategy, family plan or business investment is the maintenance. Maintenance entails hard work and commitment. You can't just buy the car and expect it to keep up itself. You can't mow the lawn one week and expect it to magically remain perfectly cut for the next three months. You have to maintain it. You have to sustain it. In the same way, after you make the turn, you must learn to maintain what you have on the one hand, and not be afraid to go beyond what you've maintained on the other. Healthy marriages succeed because both parties are committed to keeping the relationship fresh. Churches and businesses grow only if the leader is willing to assess the process and expand on the vision when necessary. If a visionary has a progressive mentality and the maintenance to keep their vision going, then he or she has mastered the secret to making pivotal turns that will produce right outcomes. Innovation does not always come in the new. Sometimes it comes by simply reshaping what is old.

> *Innovation does not always come in the new. Sometimes it comes by simply reshaping what is old.*

Disney World is one of the greatest examples of good maintenance and progressive vision. In one single invention, Walter Elias Disney balanced tradition and modernity all in one. He was born with a love for cartoon figures and graphic arts, but

Turning Point

he made the turn in 1955 when he invested in a $17 million project called Magic Kingdom. From there he expanded that vision to create Walt Disney World. It took 52 months to build and seven years to plan. The land he purchased was twice the size of Manhattan Island (43 square miles to be exact), and on October 1, 1971, Disney was opened to the public.

Undoubtedly, this project took commitment and innovation, but the key to Disney's legendary creation depended on the maintenance. This mastermind not only developed an amusement park, hotel resort vacation center, and a "Community of Tomorrow" in the same year, but he also knew how to measure if one part of the vision became outdated. He expanded and updated his vision frequently and before he knew it, Walt Disney began to attract kings, presidents, and leaders from all across the globe.

> *Cater your plan toward primary and secondary audiences. Visions must progress with people.*

Decades later, the vision is still blooming. According to a 2006 financial report, The Walt Disney Company reported $34 billion in revenue. This figure increases exponentially by the year because parents, church groups and camps of every ethnic representation, have bought into this vision. Every day, at different times of the year, families pack up cars to take their loved ones to the historic Disney World. Why? How was Disney able to re-invent the wheel time and time again?

Some may argue that Disney had a love for kids, and he knew how to keep the attention of children. But I believe that the secret was in attracting the parents as well. Indeed, parents expect the children to have a good time, but the reality is, parents enjoy the experience of Disney World just as much as their children.

The point is this: if you're going to become the next Walt Disney, learn how to bring your vision up to date. Cater your plan toward primary audiences and secondary audiences. VISIONS

Be a Progressive Visionary

MUST PROGRESS WITH PEOPLE. Visions must mature over time. Which means, you cannot be afraid to enhance something within the vision in order for the vision to be considered current. You can still have new ideas with a vintage vision. We see "makeover maintenance" all of the time, but we do not realize it. How many times have artists done a remake of a song? How many times have we heard "Amazing Grace" arranged and re-arranged? The movie *Karate Kid* was only one example of a classic movie remake that succeeded in the 21st century as much as it did in the 20th century.

When it comes to our personal vision, we must think the same way. I know you might be scared to update it because you think you're not being true to it (especially if your vision carries a family name or tradition), but the truth is, visions must reflect the NOW and not hang on the THEN. Once a vision becomes dated, its audience dies. And when an audience loses interest, your vision depreciates. The people who created the blueprints for it may want to see dinosaurs, but in the age in which we live, dinosaurs only attract people who like *Jurassic Park*. But even *Jurassic Park* is an excellent example of what it means to keep your audience interested by modernizing a vision that seems extinct.

Keep your audience wanting to come back for more! Keep your ideas fresh. Maintenance in this instance means that you have assessed the audience and concluded that more people want to see the future instead of exploring the past.

This was the trait that differentiated David from his son, Solomon. Surely, Solomon did not have the spirit of David. No one could out-worship David. But at the same time, David did not have the progressive mindset of Solomon. Solomon was a thinker. Solomon was wise. He thought differently than any one and every one around his time. As a result, Solomon introduced international trade, stock, import and export, partnership, and monopoly to the world. He saw the world beyond the view of his father but within the scope of the same God who led them both.

In other words, this was not a criticism of David. It was actually a compliment because Solomon could not have seen what he saw unless he was standing on his fathers' shoulders.

Solomon was likened to the Vanderbilt family. Cornelius Vanderbilt, upon his death, left most of his $100 million estate to his eldest son, William Henry. William Henry, then, assumed responsibility for the family empire and doubled the assets. In 1881, William built a 59-room mansion at 640 Fifth Avenue. It was the largest house in Manhattan. But the story doesn't end there. When the house was completed, only one of William's children resided in the home. His name was George Vanderbilt. George continued to build the family empire and traveled to Europe, Asia, and Africa each year (beginning at age 10). On one of his traveling trips, he stumbled upon the mountains of Asheville, North Carolina; and went on to own and design America's largest home on a 125,000-acre estate. The architect, Richard Morris Hunt, designed the Biltmore house, which sits on 4 acres of floor space and consists of 250 rooms, 34 bedrooms, 43 bathrooms, and 65 fireplaces. What's more, the house has a swimming pool, gymnasium, changing rooms, a bowling alley, servants' quarters, and multiple kitchens in the basement alone!

The question is simple: whose shoulders are you standing on? How has your vision grown since the time you've started? Like Solomon, your vision must exceed the generations that have preceded you. If a billionaire passes on his earnings to his son and his son dies with a billion dollars, he has failed his father. He has also failed himself because as an inheritor of a great vision, it is our responsibility to take what we are given and move up to the next level. In order to be great, you must despise being good.

CHAPTER THIRTY-TWO

Be Balanced

"Life is like riding a bicycle. To keep your balance you must keep moving."
-Albert Einstein

His name was Karl Wallenda. Founder of the internationally known daredevil circus and the creator of "The Flying Wallendas." This family of entertainers put on death-defying stunts without safety nets, cycled on high wires, and developed the three-tier 7-Man-Pyramid. I guess you can say they loved to walk on the wild side. But please do not misunderstand: they knew what they were doing. Our "wild" was their "norm." Our "never" was there "usual." They were no amateurs. Their expertise was balance. They had precise balance all of the time, and if ever they found themselves in a compromising situation, they knew what to do to avoid falling.

So impressive were these boys that Wallenda, at the age of 65, performed a high-wire walk across the Tallulah River in 1970. There was an audience of 30,000 watching, and if that wasn't pressure enough, Wallenda decided to do two headstands as he crossed the quarter-mile-wide gap!

Eight years later, however, Wallenda would not go down in history for his record-breaking stunts or his incredible performances with the Ringling Brothers & Barnum and Bailey Circus. Instead, he made history for having an untimely death. Wallenda was now 73 years old, and attempted to walk between the two towers of the historic Condado Plaza Hotel in Puerto Rico. 121 feet above pavement. Film crews were taping, and of course, onlookers were looking. No safety net or plan B in place. This was a piece of cake for an expert in tightrope. On this

Turning Point

particular day, however, the winds were a little too strong and Karel Wallenda lost his balance, fell, and died instantly.

I don't know if "professional tight ropers" are reading this book, but even if you do not plan to walk across two high-rise buildings, the point is: you're never too old to learn more balance. Everything you do must be balanced. Your eating habits, your career choices, your personal plans, family goals and mental health, must be balanced.

> *...you're never too old to learn more balance. Everything you do must be balanced.*

Whenever you make a decision to make the turn, know that you are standing in two places at the same time. You are standing in the strength of where you are and you are standing in the focus of where you are going. Strength and focus will balance us all. If I stand in the strength of where I am, then I don't lose my base and my foundation. I don't forget where I've come from. But if my other foot is positioned toward where I'm headed, then my future will eventually become my base. So in a sense, I will always be positioned toward progress because each time I walk, one foot takes me toward focus, and the other keeps me strong enough now to make good progress later.

What are you doing now?
What does NOW mean to you?

In order to maintain balance, ask yourself: What is my now? Where am I headed? How will my NOW change when I get there? Your now is just as important as your later. No matter how many achievements you accumulate, continue to define your "now." What did "now" mean before and after the turn? How does your now differ from others around you? No doubt, your now must be uniquely different from everyone else because someone else's NOW could actually be your THEN. While you are getting

Be Balanced

onto a flight, someone else is getting off. Now is different for everyone.

Let's look at it from this angle. Someone twenty years old knows all of the latest electronic gadgets that exist, and they are probably using them now. Meanwhile, someone who is a senior in age, may be learning how to set up an email address now. Both age groups are active and present at this particular time, but their now is different. You've got no business trying to operate like a senior if you are technologically savvy. At the same time, no matter how much of an expert you are in tightrope, you don't need to find yourself walking across two buildings at 78 years of age; especially if there is no safety net! All the balance and experience in the world cannot stop the aging process. Make sure that what you do NOW is true to the time in which you live. Know when your time is up and compensate for "unexpected winds." What makes a great team is when a player knows when to become a great coach.

The next thing you must do, as you work to maintain balance, is resist all pettiness. Do not allow yourself to magnify the petty. Focus on your goals and do not let the winds of distraction cause you to waver. If you are goal-oriented and destiny driven, you won't allow petty people, petty places, and petty things to pollute your perception. Why? Because paying attention to petty things actually destroys prosperous people.

How many times have we delayed our lives on arguments that didn't matter? How many times have we found ourselves distracted by people who were not even in our vision? How many times have we looked at ourselves and said, "Had I not listened to the lie that I thought I was love, I may have found this sooner?" Do not magnify the petty. Petty things are only designed to make you think they matter, but if it was really as important, then it wouldn't need to advertise itself so much. If a person intends to partner with you, you will know it; without them begging or pleading. *Don't magnify the petty*. You've got to stay balanced and focused. I can't tell you how many people I know who will allow ten minutes of a negative moment to spoil 24 hours in a day simply because they magnified the negative.

The parable of the prodigal son tells of an overlooked brother who magnified the petty. He had everything he needed to survive in his father's house, but he allowed jealousy to distract him when his brother returned home. He magnified a simple party that the father had thrown and began to interpret his father's gifts to one son as symbolic of his lesser value toward the other. The prodigal was only being celebrated for his return. The other brother should've focused on his faithfulness. He was a consistent help to his father. He was always there. The other brother was coming back to a place where the faithful brother was. He had the right to become upset, but if your anger takes you to the point that you forget your purpose, you may destroy your destiny. You may give up your birthright simply because you failed to see the bigger picture.

Do not magnify the petty. Don't allow your prodigal brother to downgrade your value from maturity to immaturity. Never allow anything or anyone to have that kind of power in your life. You are the older brother/sister for a reason. The younger one has come back to learn from you!

Keep looking ahead and when all else fails, ask for a safety net! Be balanced.

Chapter Thirty-Three

Be Disciplined

"Discipline is the bridge between goals and accomplishments."
-Jim Rohn

I can remember a long time ago looking at a gymnast compete in the Olympics. She was an excellent competitor who knew how to stretch her body beyond stretchable means. I watched her and I studied as she perfectly expanded her legs and flipped with one arm and then quickly leapt into a spin-off on one hand! She would do it again and again and again. Each time, she would land solidly on her feet. With one leg she'd spin and within seconds, her entire body would swing around the floor mat with perfect alignment. As I watched her, I remember thinking to myself, "Sometimes I have trouble walking with two legs and here this lady is suspending her entire body on one arm! This is crazy." But it wasn't crazy. It was good technique; and it took years of training. What she presented to millions that day was nothing more than a routine she had practiced and prepared over time. It certainly didn't happen overnight. It took discipline.

How do I know? Well, after I saw this fantastic competition, I was inspired to try it myself. I stretched my legs and moved all of the furniture. I wanted to make sure there was ample room for me to "do my thing" because I'm a little heavier than the gymnast. On top of that, I prayed for the Lord to help me align myself the right way; according to his will. And after three failed attempts, I made a final assessment—I don't have the discipline it takes to do this. Then I realized something else as a result of this failed effort: you can never have the discipline to do anything that is not your vision.

This principle taught me more about discipline than all the

athletic trainers in the gym could have ever taught me. Discipline is the key to consistency, but your discipline key must fit inside of your destiny door. Only certain kinds of doors will unlock your best potential. There is a door of vision and a pathway of purpose specifically designed for you to go through. Stop trying to walk through other people's doors! Find your door and make sure your key fits!

I believe one of the reasons most of us fail is not because we lack the initiative—it's because we are wasting our energy putting the key through the wrong door. Let's be honest. Lack of discipline and trying out keys that don't fit are two reasons we get into the struggles we found ourselves in. Bad relationships, bad business deals, and bad church experiences have left us feeling as if there is no hope after faith has run out. But there is hope! If there is life, then there is hope! You've made the turn already; so now you must reroute your discipline so that it coincides with the right thing and the right people. If you do not, you will end up making a double u-turn out of your turn. You could also end up in the hospital because you weren't fit to be anybody's Olympian in the first place!

> *Lack of discipline and trying out keys that don't fit are two reasons we get into the struggles we found ourselves in.*

Here are a few "must know's" about discipline that are absolutely imperative for your continued success.

1. Be consistent and disciplined in gaining new information regularly. In this age, information changes almost daily. If you visit cnn.com ten minutes after you first checked it, you'll read an entirely different article than what was previously posted. No one in the 21st Century has time to try out old ideas. Discipline begins with an unwillingness to marry what you are most familiar with, to the point that you destroy the new data, research, and information that can help make your job easier.

2. Be careful not to overwork for others and under-work

Be Disciplined

your mind. What do I mean by this? Quite simple. Many times we spend a great deal of time working hard on making everything and everybody around us happy. We overwork for others and try to accommodate every one else, and in the meantime, the thing that brings us success or satisfaction gets malnourished. We become exasperated when it's finally time to develop our plan or grow our vision all because we are not giving the necessary attention to the vision or the idea itself. Never let your vision get the crumbs from your cake. You deserve the first slice! If you are disciplined and aware, then you will never put more energy into other people's visions than you do your own. You will learn how to allocate time for yourself and your family, instead of burning out trying to counsel everyone else's problems. You'll be surprised to know how many professional counselors have counselors themselves. Mind you, they have a degree and are professionally trained—and still, the weight of other people's baggage can weigh on them to the point that they now find themselves depressed and detached. Don't let it happen!

3. Know the difference between loyalty and commitment. To be loyal is to go to work every day. To be committed is to do the work when you get there. Don't reward loyalty when it is not matched with commitment. No matter the circumstance—if you have employees working for you, make sure to harmonize loyalty and commitment. If you are the employer and the employee (which means you are the one rewarding yourself), stay true to your discipline. Force yourself to marry loyalty and commitment. If you do, you will holistically become a person of discipline no matter what you commit to. You won't need a paycheck, an annual bonus or prominence to pump you up into motivation. Discipline will already serve you the fuel you need to succeed.

4. Never look for people to be excited about what you see! Always remember a vision is for you to manifest and for everybody else to enjoy. The building of a vision is for your eyes only (along with those who are working with you). This requires discipline for many reasons. Sometimes we do not fill out the

proper psychological application before we share information to people who should not be privy to that information. Your discipline begins when you stop telling all of your friends about your dreams.

Joseph's brothers could not handle him. Neither can some of the people around you. Be disciplined enough to pray before you share. Everyone will not be excited. Everyone will not pat you on the back. And sometimes, it's not because people are "hating on your vision" (sometimes they are); but most times, hindsighters will never be able to see like foresighters. In other words, some people will never see as far as your vision will go simply because it's not their vision to see! I always tell members of my church this: one way to tell if you should share information with someone is based on how they react to good news. How someone reacts to your little joys will indicate how they respond to your greater joys. If someone is always trying to discourage you away from the big picture, they can't handle your dream. If they are always trying to steer you away from what you know God has called you to do, then chances are, they can't see it. Another possibility is that they *can* see it, but they don't want you to do anything greater than what they are going to do. They have a superiority complex. No one around them can outdo them. Everyone else's house needs to be smaller. Your job needs to pay less. Your ministry needs to be a little less successful than the guy giving you all the advice.

From these people, you must flee! Discipline yourself to be your own support system when people begin to shift (because they will shift). You are great because God's greatness is within you. If people can't see you as great, it's probably because they don't even see themselves as great!

Discipline is key. In all things, exercise discipline. Use the right key to open the right doors. Carve out time for just your vision and your vision only. Be committed and be loyal. And finally, be careful about those with whom you share your dream.

Chapter Thirty-Four

Be Healthy and Rest!
"The first wealth is health."
-Ralph Waldo Emerson

Thank you Ralph Waldo Emerson for the famous words, "the first wealth is health." Indeed, this is truer now than ever before. Every year, churches are losing pastors to heart attacks and strokes that no one saw coming. Families are losing heads of households all because mama wouldn't check her cholesterol intake and papa hadn't had a physical exam since high school football tryouts. Children are being diagnosed as if they are senior citizens, and senior citizens are outliving their children! How can this be? What is going on in the world?

I cannot tell you how many people I meet on a day-to-day basis who are walking time bombs. They have money but they aren't able to enjoy it because they are battling a sickness that could've been prevented. They love life but they can't take time off because they are living paycheck to paycheck. Or, they are on the road toward success and then all of a sudden, the flat tire of an unexpected doctor's report takes them by surprise.

When is the last time you took the time to check on you?
When is the last time you treated yourself to a day at the spa?
When is the last vacation you've taken?

How many times can you recall going to the doctor for a check-up, and not just when you felt pain in your body?

These are questions I need you to interrogate frequently. I am no Dr. Oz, but I do know how essential it is for you to maintain good health.

Turning Point

This is the next "Now What" nugget you need to be aware of: REST and RELAXATION. Yes! After you have turned and after you have made good decisions with good perception and proper reinvention, you must not forget the importance of rest and health. A healthy person creates a healthy vision. A healthy person maintains a healthy lifestyle. Take it from me: if you don't take care of you, the vision can't take care of you. If the family is dependent upon you to do everything for them, what will they do without you? Exercise, eating properly and rest are three necessary elements as you decide to go from good to great. If you want to be alive to see the fruit your tree will harvest, then you'd better rest up every once in a while! Why would you accomplish so much and die before you can enjoy it?

> *If you want to be alive to see the fruit your tree will harvest, then you'd better rest up every once in a while!*

According to a recent study done by the National Health and Nutrition Examination Survey, one third of the adults in America are obese. What is most disturbing, however, is that most of this unfortunate obesity stems from unhealthy eating habits. Which means, we actually can live a healthier life if we refrain from a few things; we just choose not to. Every family reunion or high school reunion, we splurge. Every Sunday after church, we indulge! Every time we see our favorite dessert pastry, we run straight for the sugar and whip cream! Don't ever say you'll never commit suicide if you're not taking care of your body.

Consider your body. Make a decision to be healthy and stay healthy at all costs. I've seen many runners start out very quickly but unable to finish the race due to exhaustion and depletion. The same is true for visionaries with a booming business idea or a bountiful congregation. Depending on the kind of vision you have and the size of the success you can foresee, it will take a level of energy from you that cannot be compromised or overlooked. All visions need energy to accomplish them. All ideas need time to

Be Healthy and Rest!

breathe and grow. If you don't take care of yourself, you become the murderer of your own vision. You become the only assassin in the room. You become the death sentence that your body never thought would happen so soon.

Another way you can damage your future is by obsessing over your goals and aspirations. If you don't learn to leave your vision alone sometimes, you'll become overly consumed with it and before long, you'll be messing up an already perfect cake batter. The worst kind of recipe is one that someone takes too much time to cook! The process of achievement must include time away from that which you aspire to achieve. If you want to be married, it's a great thing to meet other people; but every once in a while, take a Sabbath from the social gatherings and just enjoy spending time with you. If you're up all night working on a paper, there is no way you will be able to read the words clearly if you find yourself drinking your fifth cup of coffee! Step away and let rest have her perfect work.

Be healthy and rest—it's the only way to maintain success. Sometimes, you've got to step away from what you love the most so that you are not consumed by it. You can't allow it to suffocate you. You can't allow your loved ones to rule over every business decision you make. If you don't choose to create some space between you and your vision, then pretty soon your joy will turn into a job; and when that happens, the spirit of it has lost its life.

---

3 John 1:2 Beloved, I wish above all things that thou mayest prosper and be in health, even as thy soul prospereth.

Chapter Thirty-Five

Be a Dreamer

"Happy are those who dream dreams and are ready to pay the price to make them come true."
-Leon Joseph Cardinal Suenens

I must say, I have driven a lot of beautiful cars in my life. I am grateful for the exposure and at one point in time, I used to be extremely excited about new releases, car shows, and luxury vehicles. But if I can be honest, trucks and cars don't really move me anymore. They don't excite me because I've been blessed to drive the best. Everything I've ever wanted to drive in, I've already seen or driven; that is, until I found myself in Beverly Hills, California a few months ago.

It was beautiful. It was futuristic. I had never seen this class or model before. Here I am: in a city I don't live in, on a street I don't know, in a rental car that I no longer want to ride in. I turn my car around and I slow down long enough to parallel my car next to another car. I am staring at this gorgeous vehicle. It captured my attention. It drew me in.

Within minutes, I find myself doing something that I never thought I'd do again—I dreamed that I was in it. I dreamed that I was the owner of this vehicle. And if I –a man who doesn't obsess over cars—was able to dream that I was in it, then the creator of this vehicle fulfilled his or her dream that day.

You have accomplished your vision when other people can see themselves as a part of what began as an idea in your head. You have succeeded when your vision causes others to dream. But, this is only the beginning. Sure, you have learned a few essential components you need to achieve success. Yes, you have achieved greatness and you are grateful for the blessings you have received. But now, it's time to dream again. It's time to turn these principles into stepping-stones. It's time to go higher and reach beyond your new norm. In order for you to maintain success, you must see maintenance as a mountainous journey. You can never be fully satisfied with where you are. You must always be reaching for the prize toward the higher calling. There is a higher calling. There is a bigger idea in you; which is why you must dream again.

Your next turn will define the shift of a century. Your next turn may just reconstruct the way people understand politics or international relations. Your ideas and dreams must introduce to this world the reason why we live. Why? Because you have within you the next wonder of the world. You have within you the cure to AIDS or the resolution to gang violence. You have it within you! But in order to activate and manifest that dream, it must leave your mind and begin to influence others.

> *In order to activate and manifest that dream, it must leave your mind and begin to influence others.*

When you dream, your mind expands, but when you wake up from the dream and remember it, you have begun to re-envision. And when you walk into what you envision, then you have moved into the manifestation of that vision. This is the cycle of a visionary. This is the way to continue making the right kind of turn.

Let me end by giving you a few unforgettable principles for success. First, make sure your ideas introduce to this world the reason why we live. Make sure your purpose in life is to help someone else live better. Make it clear by your life, the reason why you refuse to be held in a box; the reason why children want to go to Disney world; the reason why discrimination, ageism, or sexism will have no ability to block you from success. When the road gets difficult, remember that you have a dream. It has never been done until you do it. It has never been dreamt until you dream it. It has never been experienced until you smile after you think about it.

Be a Dreamer

When you get there, you have just arrived to your next turning point.

Second, no matter what the economy may dictate or what a guidance counselor may say, there is no such thing as "CAN NOT BE DONE." The only question you need to answer is: do I know enough dreamers connected to enough thinkers to make it happen? If the inventors of modern technology really believed that everything that could be done was already done, then we would still be driving 1984 Corvette's and listening to 8-track tapes. The world is waiting on another dreamer to break the glass ceiling. The world is waiting on another moon walker.

It was the United States that went to the moon at a time when the world was not as technologically advanced as we currently are. Now, we have a difficult time orbiting the Earth. That tells me something important. Obviously, someone is thinking too hard and not dreaming enough. Someone is tracking too much history and not thinking about the future. Everything—and I do mean everything— is doable. It is accomplish-able. What makes a great dreamer great is his or her fearlessness. You can do this! God is with you! Don't rob the world because you're scared to dream. We need you to invent, think, create, and make only what God has given you the ability to do. He did not expect for it to go back in the Earth at your death—that's why He brought you out of the earth to make it happen.

What is the key question for a dreamer? The key question is only two words long—What if? If people cannot take your "what if," then they cannot take your dream. After you finish reading, walk away dreaming. As you dream aloud, ask yourself "What if?"

What if the richest man in the world is not the richest?
What if the greatest gold mine has not yet been found?
What if archeologists have not found the greatest treasure?
What if I can build the biggest office in my own city?
What if I am the curse breaker of my family?

──────── Turning Point ────────

What if I can accomplish a better time than any Olympian?
What if the greatest book has not been written?
What if the biggest diamond is still in the dirt looking for someone to find it?
What if the best fuel has not been discovered?
What if the cure to every disease is still out there in the leaf of a plant?
What if?
What if the mind that can do this... *is reading this book right now?*

Coming Soon 2011

In this book, Kevin Williams will discuss 10 Things Every MAN and WOMAN Battles with.

For more information visit
www.drkevinawilliams.com
www.godzchildproductions.net
| 877.777.7016 |